Second Chance:

A Journey of Self-Discovery and Personal-Growth

New York City Books
www.nycitybooks.com

217 Peace Pipe Way
Georgetown TX 78628 USA

Printed in the United States of America

Publisher's Cataloging-in-Publication data
Arat, Mel
Second Chance: A Journey of Self-Discovery and Personal-Growth

I-ISBN: 9781088031254

LCCN: 2023908605

Second Chance:

A Journey of Self-Discovery and Personal-Growth

Mel ARAT

New York City Books

"In Second Chance, Mel Arat delivers a powerful message about the importance of embracing the opportunities life presents us with. With a compelling writing style and poignant personal anecdotes, Arat inspires readers to see past their mistakes and move forward towards a brighter future. This book is a must-read for anyone who wants to achieve personal growth and success." -
Elissa Siegel-Author of Recognition

"Second Chance is a masterpiece that beautifully captures the essence of the human experience. Arat's writing is a combination of vulnerability, strength, and wisdom that will leave readers feeling inspired and motivated to embrace their second chances. I highly recommend this book to anyone who wants to take control of their life and create the future they deserve."
Necdet Buyukbay-International Business Consultant

Second Chance
Life is a journey, long and winding,
Full of ups and downs, twists and turning,
With second chances, hope abounding,
A new path, a fresh start, we're learning.

A second chance, a new beginning,
A chance to mend, a chance to grow,
A chance to see the light, winning,
And to rise up, from the shadows.

With each mistake, comes a lesson,
A chance to learn, a chance to grow,
With each failure, comes progression,
A chance to rise, a chance to glow.

So if you've stumbled, in your journey,
And feel like all is lost,
Remember, a second chance is waiting,
For you to seize, at any cost.

With faith and courage, in your heart,
And a vision, clear and bright,
A second chance, can be the start,
Of a brand new, shining light.

CONTENTS

Introduction

Life is an unpredictable journey filled with moments of joy and moments of hardship. At times, we may find ourselves in situations that we never thought we would be in, perhaps as a result of our own choices or circumstances beyond our control. In such situations, it's easy to feel like we have reached a dead-end or that we have failed. However, life is not a one-time deal; we are given second chances.

Second chances come in many forms, whether it's a new job opportunity after being fired, a chance to mend a broken relationship, or an opportunity to start fresh in a new place. It's a chance to learn from our mistakes, improve ourselves, and grow as individuals. Second chances provide us with hope that there is always the possibility of a better future, no matter how difficult our past may have been.

In this book, we will explore the concept of second chances in life. We will examine the various ways in which second chances can manifest themselves, the benefits of embracing them, and the challenges that come with them. We will also delve into the role of forgiveness and acceptance in moving forward, and how to make the most of second chances to achieve our goals.

Using real-life stories, personal anecdotes, and expert insights, this book aims to provide readers with a deeper understanding of the importance of second chances in life. It serves as a reminder that no matter how tough life may get, we always have the opportunity to make things right and start anew. Whether you are currently facing a challenging situation or looking for inspiration to take your life to the next level, this book will provide you with the tools to embrace second chances and create the life you deserve.

The concept of second chances is something that we all desire, especially when we have experienced failure or setbacks in life. The idea of being given another opportunity to try again is comforting, and it's easy to see why it's so appealing.

However, second chances aren't always readily available, and we must use them wisely. In today's world, where we are experiencing significant changes, carrying our past habits into the present and future can cause problems. Therefore, the concept of second chances becomes even more critical.

It's also important to note that even those who have achieved significant success may still want to do things differently if given another opportunity. Life offers different alternatives, and we may be happier and more successful if we choose another path. This is why successful individuals or organizations also need a second chance.

The crucial question is, can we use our second chances effectively? In many cases, we repeat the same actions that led to our failures and don't make any changes. To make the most of a second chance, we must try new and different things to get different results. This is the only way to learn from our past mistakes and grow.

Lastly, it's essential to recognize that while we desire a second chance for ourselves, we may not always be generous in giving others the same opportunity. This is a contradiction that needs to be resolved, particularly in the business world, where second chances are often given over a certain period.

In conclusion, second chances are a crucial concept, especially in times of change. They offer us the opportunity to try again, learn from our mistakes, and grow. We must use them effectively, be open to trying new things, and be willing to give others the same opportunity. By doing so, we can all learn from our past mistakes, grow, and achieve greater success.

Chapter 1 Understanding the Second Chances in Life

Life is a journey filled with ups and downs, twists and turns, and unexpected surprises. Along the way, we face challenges and make mistakes, and at times, we may feel like we have hit a dead-end. However, life is not a one-time deal, and we are often given a second chance to try again.

The concept of second chance is not just about getting another opportunity to try again; it's also about embracing the lessons learned from past mistakes, improving oneself, and making the most of the opportunities presented. Second chances come in different forms, and it's up to us to recognize them and take advantage of them.

In this chapter, we will explore the concept of second chance and what it means for us. We will look at how it differs from the idea of starting over and why it's essential to embrace second chances in life. We will also examine how second chances can bring about positive change, personal growth, and transformation.

To begin, let's differentiate between the concepts of second chance and starting over. Starting over implies completely abandoning the past and beginning anew with a fresh slate. In contrast, a second chance acknowledges the past mistakes, learns from them, and improves upon them to move forward. Starting over may seem like the easy way out, but it doesn't necessarily address the root cause of the problem. A second chance offers an opportunity for growth and self-improvement.

Second chances are vital because they allow us to break free from the negative patterns that have held us back in the past. We can choose to embrace the new opportunities presented and make positive changes to our lives. This can lead to personal growth and transformation, as we learn from our past mistakes and strive to be better versions of ourselves.

Moreover, second chances can also benefit others around us. Forgiving someone and giving them a second chance can be transformative, both for the person receiving the opportunity and for the relationship as a whole. It's essential to recognize that second chances are not just about ourselves, but they also offer the possibility of repairing broken relationships and strengthening bonds with others.

In conclusion, the concept of second chance is essential for personal growth and transformation. It's not just about getting another opportunity to try again, but it's about acknowledging our past mistakes, learning from them, and making positive changes to our lives. Second chances offer an opportunity to break free from negative patterns, repair relationships, and transform our lives for the better. By embracing second chances, we can create a brighter future for ourselves and those around us.

The Second Chance That Wasn't: John's Tale of Wasted Opportunities

After graduating from a prestigious American university, John landed a job at a large company and entered the business world with enthusiasm. However, his enthusiasm died out as quickly as a spark. Six months into his job, he became indifferent to his work and failed to complete his projects on time. Although the company was large, John's poor performance went unnoticed among thousands of employees. Although he did not lose his job in three years, he was not a star in any manager's eyes, so his chances of advancement in the company were slim.

Meanwhile, his old friend from the neighborhood, Mike, had a good business idea but wanted a partner to join him. John was a good candidate, having graduated from one of the country's leading universities in business administration and three years of experience working for one of the largest companies in the industry. John saw this as a great second chance to make up for his lost opportunity. Initially, he put in a star performance, arriving early, meeting with employees, and planning production. The company secured its first customers, and orders were coming in, with John taking responsibility for the production process.

Unfortunately, after a few months, John's momentum waned, and he began arriving late to work and paying less attention to production and procurement. He was withdrawing money from the company's account to fund his personal enjoyment, including an expensive car and a luxurious rental house in an upscale neighborhood. Meanwhile, Mike, the owner of the business idea, was working tirelessly from the outset. John's poor work ethic became a concern, and Mike warned him several times, but there was no positive change in his behavior. At the end of the first year, Mike asked John to sell his shares and leave the company. John agreed to leave, saying, "I don't stay where I am not wanted."

Ten years later, Mike's business had grown into a large factory with over a hundred employees. In contrast, John had joined many companies, often saying he could do a great job, but he worked for a short time in many of them.

Looking at John's story, we see that he recklessly wasted all the opportunities that came his way. Not only did he fail to work hard enough at his first job, but he also failed to take advantage of the significant opportunity that followed. Instead of taking responsibility for his failures, he would likely blame the employers, managers, or work environment for leaving those jobs.

From Failure to Triumph: Blake's Story of Dedication

Blake was in the process of preparing for the SAT exam to gain admission to a prestigious college. However, the study materials and practice exams were proving to be too much for her. She didn't prepare sufficiently and ultimately received a poor score. Blake requested an additional year to prepare for the SAT exam, and her family didn't hesitate to grant her wish. She enrolled in a prep course again with the intention of using her second chance to either prepare properly or risk missing out on college again. Blake made the decision to take her second chance seriously and take on the responsibilities that came with it. She significantly reduced her time on the social media, despite the challenge of waking up early in the morning. She tracked her progress by independently solving past SAT questions and concentrating on the areas where she needed improvement. Even when her family suggested going skiing during Christmas break, she declined and continued to study at home. In the end, she took the SAT exam again and, despite feeling unsure about her performance, she discovered that she was in the top 1% percentile. She was accepted into all three colleges she had applied to.

When analyzing Blake's story, we can see that after her initial poor SAT exam results, she made a significant behavioral change and dedicated herself to preparing for the exam the second time around. Using a second chance doesn't always guarantee a favorable outcome, but it does mean continuing to move forward and persevering towards achieving one's goals.

Story of Cane: From Partygoer to Honors Graduate

Cane thrived in college life, enjoying the many cafes around campus and playing card games. He was popular among the young women and was frequently invited to parties and events. However, his love for the social scene led him to miss classes, and he eventually got expelled from school. He was in disbelief and unable to tell his family about his situation. Feeling lost and directionless, Cane stopped talking to his old friends and decided to retake the entrance exam.

He successfully got into the Russian Language and Literature program with his language score, not having to retake classes he had already completed before his expulsion. Cane made significant changes in his life, cutting back on socializing and focusing on his studies. He was determined to succeed, even ordering books on learning Russian and joke books from Russia. He received a scholarship to attend the Pushkin Institute in Moscow, where he practiced his Russian every summer until he graduated.

By the end of his fourth year, Cane's Russian language skills were as strong as his native language, and he graduated with honors. His family and friends were amazed at the transformation in his determination and work ethic. Cane continued his academic pursuits, obtaining an MBA degree with honors.

Cane's story is a testament to the power of a second chance. Although he wasn't aware of his actions until he got expelled from school, he used his second chance to work hard and make a significant behavioral change. His dedication to his studies and willingness to make changes resulted in a remarkable international performance.

The Story of Tim: Turning Setbacks into Success

Tim, a student in the English department, was a sociable and ambitious individual who started looking for work in New York City. He landed his first job as a salesman, but despite claiming to have sold all the goods in the first month, he was fired when none of the accounts could be collected. He then worked in accounting, but was fired again when the accounts got mixed up. He was fired from his third job for calling the General Manager "bro" instead of "sir," and from his fourth job for sleeping at his desk. Despite being fired from multiple jobs, he persisted and went through 15 different jobs until he finished school.

Together with two friends, Tim opened a small tutoring center that taught physics and mathematics. However, the partnership fell apart due to issues with sharing profits. Tim then hired a physics and mathematics teacher, but they struggled to find enough students. He hired Xena, a girl, to find new students, and the physics and mathematics teachers quit due to not being paid. Xena, a new marketing manager, suggested that Tim, with his English degree, should be teaching English instead of physics and math. This idea sparked Tim's mind, and he transformed the tutoring center into an English language school.

People had a positive image of Tim since he was a successful student about to graduate at NYU. After enrolling many students, he hired new teachers and opened several branches of an English language school in New York.

In Tim's story, the change he made at his seventeenth job ultimately led to a positive outcome. Despite experiencing setbacks in his previous jobs, his latest opportunity was actually his second chance - the one he pursued after his previous attempt. Tim's story serves as a reminder that failure does not define a person, and success can be achieved through perseverance and a willingness to adapt and try new approaches.

The Story of Identical Twins' Different Destinies

Nadir, a resident of Mardin, had longed for children with his family. After years of struggle, they finally welcomed identical twin girls, Aise and Fatima. The parents were overjoyed to have the children they had hoped for, but tragedy struck before the girls turned one. In a car accident, both parents were killed, leaving the babies orphaned. The girls' mother had two sisters, one in Istanbul and the other in a village in Mardin. The aunts took on the responsibility of caring for the twins, with Aise going to Istanbul and Fatima to the village in Mardin. The identical twins were now going to grow up separately.

Aise's aunt in Istanbul was a kind and loving woman who treated Aise like her own daughter. Despite losing her mother, Aise had the love and support of her aunt who encouraged her every step of the way. Aise excelled in school, working hard to be the first in her class to learn to read. Despite her aunt's support, she remained introverted but used her quiet nature to think deeply.

Fatima was not as fortunate as Aise. She lived with her aunt, uncle, and their five children in a village struggling to make ends meet. Fatima was bullied by her cousins and her aunt's husband did not treat her well. She was insulted when she made mistakes and felt worthless. When she was old enough to attend school, she had to travel to a nearby school and took two years to learn to read and write. She was not given the opportunity to learn and felt like a housemaid in the household. At 16, she was married off, and her situation seemed hopeless.

Despite being identical twins, their environment shaped their outcomes more than their personality traits. Our surroundings determine what we can and cannot do in life. We can change the behavior resulting from our environment and the influence of it to change the outcomes we get. Fatima's situation in Mardin was harder than Aise's in Istanbul, and as far as the story is shared, Fatima has not yet caught her second chance. Even if Aise invites her to Istanbul, Fatima will face numerous difficulties such as adapting to the city, difficulty finding a job due to lack of education, and many more. But if Fatima can endure the pain caused by the difficulties she will face during the adaptation process, she can establish a new life. Otherwise, she will lose her second chance.

The Uninvited Guest

Sarah spotted a sparrow struggling to fly on the edge of the sidewalk. Despite flapping its wings, it couldn't get far and kept falling back down. Sarah couldn't help but feel sorry for the little bird. She initially thought to leave it be, but her conscience wouldn't let her. With a nurturing instinct, she tried to pick up the sparrow, which attempted to flee in fear. However, Sarah managed to cradle it gently like a mother would.

Concerned for the sparrow's well-being, Sarah sought out a veterinarian for assistance. On her way, she stumbled upon a pet shop and inquired about the nearest vet. Fortunately, the young man behind the counter was a veterinarian himself and offered to help Sarah. After examining the sparrow, he reassured her that the bird was not severely hurt and should recover within a week. Nonetheless, he warned that it could be dangerous for the sparrow to remain on the street as it could fall prey to a cat. The vet provided Sarah with bird feed and offered some tips on how to care for the sparrow until it could fly again, which Sarah gratefully accepted.

After a few days of care, the sparrow had regained its strength and was able to fly for four or five feets at a time. However, during one of its practice flights, the little bird flew out the window and fell to the ground since it didn't have enough energy to fly down from the fourth floor. It landed in the home of Sarah's downstairs neighbor, Mrs. Adelaide, a grumpy old woman whom everyone avoided. Sarah knocked on her door to check on the sparrow and was surprised when Mrs. Adelaide answered with a warm tone and invited her in. Sarah noticed that the sparrow was in the old woman's hands and shared her story about the bird. While the sparrow flew around the house, Sarah mentioned that many people in the apartment building were afraid of Mrs. Adelaide. In response, the old woman said, "I'm an old woman, and when people get older, they can become lonely. Sometimes, their patience wears thin, and they may become difficult with their neighbors when there's noise or the building is messy. But if people came to visit me and asked how I was doing, perhaps my tolerance towards them would improve." After this heartwarming conversation, Sarah decided to visit Mrs. Adelaide more often and even bring her to visit other neighbors.

As Sarah climbed the stairs to her apartment, she caught the attention of an elderly man who had just moved into the building. "What happened to this cute sparrow?" he asked, and they struck up a conversation. The man had a pet bird himself and was a retired English professor. During their chat, Sarah mentioned that she was struggling with English at school. When the man found out, he kindly offered to help her with her lessons for free.

When Sarah returned home with the sparrow, it was already evening. However, the mischievous bird had managed to fly into the third-floor apartment of her neighbors, Phobie and Edward, who were in the midst of a heated argument. As they were yelling at each other, the little sparrow hopped from one chair to another.

Coincidentally, Sarah knocked on their door, looking for the little bird. They invited her in, and she shared the story of the sparrow's journey, including the encounter with Mrs. Adelaide. Sarah said, "I think we forgot to listen to each other and show affection." Phoebe and Edward exchanged glances and shrugged since they realized their own situation.

The following evening, Sarah arranged a get-together, and all the neighbors brought over sweets and small gifts to visit Mrs. Adelaide. The atmosphere was incredibly heartwarming, and as they chatted, the little sparrow hopped from one chair to the next. Eventually, it flew out the window and didn't come back. Sarah's help to God's little creature had helped the whole building.

Analysis of the story

The story shows the importance of helping, both towards animals and humans, and how small acts of kindness can create a positive domino effect and a second chance for all.

It all started when Sarah saw the sparrow struggling to fly and decided to help it, even though she initially thought of walking away. Sarah's kindness towards the sparrow led her to knock on Mrs. Adelaide's door and discover that behind the old woman's grumpiness was loneliness, and her tolerance for others decreased with age. By talking to Mrs. Adelaide, Sarah learned that even difficult people can be kind if they are given a chance. This interaction with Mrs. Adelaide led Sarah to decide to visit her more often and even visit other neighbors with her, creating a ripple effect of kindness towards others.

Later, the sparrow flew into Phoebe and Edward's apartment, where they were in a heated argument. However, the presence of the sparrow and Sarah's kindness towards the bird led to a conversation about the importance of listening to each other and showing affection, which might have improved their relationship.

Finally, Sarah organized a gathering where all the neighbors visited Mrs. Adelaide with sweets and small gifts, creating a warm atmosphere and showing her that her neighbors cared for her. The presence of the sparrow, which flew from chair to chair during the gathering, brought joy and symbolized the positive domino effect of Sarah's initial act of kindness.

Overall, the story shows that helping each other can create a domino effect of positivity and create a second chance for all of us.

Field of Dreams and Second Chances

The movie "Field of Dreams"[1] is a story about a farmer named Ray Kinsella who hears a voice telling him, "If you build it, he will come." Believing that he needs to build a baseball field in the middle of his cornfield, Ray sets out to do just that, even though he has no idea why or who will come. As the story unfolds, Ray comes to understand the significance of his actions and the people he meets along the way.

One of the main themes in the movie is the concept of second chances. Ray's father died before they could reconcile their relationship, and Ray is given a chance to reconnect with him through a series of events that take place on the baseball field. Additionally, Shoeless Joe Jackson, who was banned from baseball for his involvement in the 1919 Black Sox Scandal, is given a chance to redeem himself by playing on the field that Ray built.

---

[1] Robinson, Phil Alden, dir. Field of Dreams. Universal Pictures, 1989.

Throughout the movie, we see examples of characters helping one another. Ray's wife, Annie, supports him in his seemingly crazy mission to build a baseball field. The reconnection between Ray and his father is made possible by the intervention of a mysterious doctor, Archibald "Moonlight" Graham. And Terence Mann, a once-famous author who has become a recluse, is helped by Ray, who brings him to the baseball field to experience its magic.

The domino effect of these acts of helping is profound. By building the field and bringing people together, Ray creates an opportunity for healing and redemption. The reconnection with his father allows Ray to understand the importance of family and forgiveness. Shoeless Joe's redemption shows that even those who have made mistakes can be given a second chance. And Terence Mann's experiences on the field give him a renewed sense of purpose and passion for life.

In summary, the plot of "Field of Dreams" is a story about second chances, redemption, and the power of helping others. The acts of kindness and support that are shown throughout the movie have a ripple effect that transforms the lives of those involved, creating a sense of hope and renewal.

I highly recommend watching the movie "Field of Dreams" with a lens focused on the themes of second chances and helping. This heartwarming story shows how helping others not only creates a second chance for them, but also for ourselves. Through the characters and their journeys, we see the profound impact that a helping hand can have in our own lives and the lives of those around us.

In America

In America[2], a movie by Jim Sheridan, tells the story of an Irish family that moves to New York City and struggles to adapt to their new life while dealing with personal loss. The movie portrays the theme of being honest with oneself and others. The family is

---

[2] Sheridan, Jim, dir. In America. Miramax Films, 2002.

struggling to deal with the death of their son, Frankie. Johnny, the father, is not honest with himself and pretends that his son didn't die, or never existed, which causes emotional distress to his family. This fake personality and role-playing prevent him from fully engaging with his family and allowing himself to grieve.

Furthermore, Johnny's lack of honesty and emotional vulnerability affects his audition performances. He is unable to connect with the emotions required for his acting roles and is criticized for his lack of authenticity. It is only when he finally confronts his grief and allows himself to be vulnerable that he is able to give a powerful and authentic performance. By embracing our emotions and acknowledging our vulnerabilities, we can better connect with others and achieve our goals. The theme of honesty and authenticity is woven throughout the movie, highlighting the importance of being true to oneself and working from the heart.

Seven Principles for Creating Your Second Chance

Principle 1: Take Responsibility for Your Failures
It means recognizing and owning up to your mistakes rather than blaming others for your shortcomings. By taking responsibility for your failures, you gain a sense of control over your life and are better equipped to learn from your mistakes and make improvements in the future. In the context of creating a second chance, it's important to understand that failure is a natural part of the process and taking responsibility for it is the first step towards achieving success.

John failed to take responsibility for his failures and instead blamed others for his shortcomings. To create a second chance, it's important to recognize and own up to your mistakes.

Principle 2: Persevere and Dedicate Yourself to Your Goals
To create a second chance, it's important to persevere and dedicate yourself to your goals. This means having a clear vision of what you want to achieve and committing to the necessary steps to make it happen. It also means accepting that there may be setbacks and obstacles along the way, but staying determined and continuing to work towards your goal.

After receiving poor SAT exam results, Blake dedicated herself to preparing for the exam the second time around. She persevered through the challenges of studying and took the necessary steps to improve her score. Her dedication paid off when she achieved a higher score on her second attempt, demonstrating the importance of perseverance and dedication in achieving second chances.

Principle 3: Recognize the Power of a Second Chance
This principle emphasizes the value of second chances and the transformative effect they can have on individuals. It involves recognizing the opportunities for growth and improvement that come with a fresh start and taking advantage of them. Instead of dwelling on past mistakes or failures, this principle encourages individuals to focus on the potential for positive change and to work hard towards achieving their goals.

The story of Cane illustrates the power of a second chance. Despite being expelled from school, Cane used his second chance to work hard and make a significant behavioral change. His dedication to his studies and willingness to make changes resulted in a remarkable international performance.

Principle 4: Failure Does Not Define a Person
This principle is based on the idea that failure is not an inherent characteristic of an individual and should not define them. Instead, failures should be viewed as opportunities for growth and learning.

In the text, the story of Tim exemplifies this principle. Tim faced setbacks in his previous jobs but did not allow these failures to define him. He continued to persevere and try new approaches until he found success. This principle highlights the importance of having a growth mindset and the willingness to adapt and try again after experiencing failure. By understanding that failure is not a reflection of one's character or abilities, individuals can continue to work towards their goals and achieve success.

Principle 5: Recognize the Influence of Your Environment
It is important to remember that we can still make positive changes even if our environment presents obstacles, by making conscious efforts to adapt and improve ourselves.
The story of Aise and Fatima highlights the importance of recognizing the influence of one's environment on their opportunities and outcomes. While Aise had more favorable circumstances living in Istanbul, Fatima faced greater challenges in Mardin. Understanding the role of external factors in shaping our lives can help us make more informed decisions and take actions to improve our situation.

Principle 6: Small Acts of Kindness Can Create a Ripple Effect
The sixth principle for creating a second chance is to recognize the power of small acts of kindness. The story of the sparrow in the text shows how Sarah's decision to help the bird led to a chain of events that ultimately created a positive domino effect for all involved. By being kind to the sparrow, Sarah was led to knock on Mrs. Adelaide's door, which resulted in a deeper understanding of the old woman's loneliness and a decision to visit her more often. This act of kindness towards Mrs. Adelaide led to a chain of events that brought the neighbors together and resulted in a warm atmosphere of caring and support.

The principle of small acts of kindness is powerful because it shows that even the smallest gesture can have a profound impact on someone's life. By choosing to be kind and helpful towards others, you have the potential to create a ripple effect of positivity and create a second chance for those around you.

Principle 7: Help Others and Create Opportunities for Healing and Redemption
This principle emphasizes the importance of helping others and creating opportunities for healing and redemption. By offering a helping hand and supporting those in need, we can create a ripple effect of positivity and create second chances for ourselves and others.

The act of helping others not only benefits them but also has a positive impact on our own lives, creating a sense of purpose and fulfillment.

The examples in the text, such as Sarah's act of kindness towards the sparrow and Ray's efforts to build a baseball field, show how small acts of kindness and support can transform the lives of those involved and create a sense of hope and renewal. By recognizing the power of helping others, we can create a more positive and supportive community, where everyone has a chance to succeed and thrive.

Chapter Summary

This chapter elucidates above seven crucial principles required for creating and seizing second chances in life. The initial principle emphasizes the importance of taking responsibility for personal failures, as depicted through John's story, where his inability to do so hindered his progress.

The following principle underscores the value of perseverance and dedication towards one's goals, illustrated through Blake's success in improving her SAT scores after initial failure.

Recognizing the transformative power of second chances forms the third principle.

This notion is embodied in Cane's tale, where despite his expulsion from school, he seized his second chance to excel academically on an international level.

Principle four clarifies that failure does not define a person's identity or capabilities, as represented through Tim's story. Despite setbacks, Tim remained resilient, which ultimately led to his success.

The fifth principle focuses on the influence of our environment, demonstrated through Aise and Fatima's contrasting life circumstances. Understanding these environmental impacts allows individuals to make informed decisions and work towards improving their situation.

Principle six proposes that even small acts of kindness can create a ripple effect and lead to significant positive outcomes, a concept exemplified through Sarah's decision to assist a sparrow.

Lastly, principle seven emphasizes the impact of aiding others and generating opportunities for healing and redemption. The act of supporting others benefits both the giver and receiver, leading to a more positive, supportive community where everyone can seize their second chances.

Chapter Lessons

- Taking responsibility for personal failures empowers individuals to learn and grow.
- Perseverance and dedication to one's goals can pave the way for success, even after initial setbacks.
- Acknowledging the transformative power of second chances enables individuals to focus on growth rather than dwelling on past mistakes.
- Failure should be seen as a learning opportunity rather than a definitive judgment of one's capabilities.
- Recognizing the influence of one's environment can guide more informed decision-making and proactive improvement.
- Small acts of kindness can trigger a ripple effect of positive outcomes and provide second chances for others.
- Assisting others leads to personal fulfillment and contributes to the creation of a supportive community that enables everyone to thrive.

Chapter 2 Feeling Valuable

Self-awareness and its role in the Development of Self-Confidence

Self-awareness is the ability to recognize and understand your own thoughts, feelings, and behaviors. It involves being conscious of your own strengths and weaknesses, values and beliefs, and how they shape your actions and interactions with others. Self-awareness is a key aspect of emotional intelligence and plays a crucial role in personal growth, development, and relationships. It allows individuals to gain insight into their own thought processes and behaviors, identify areas for improvement, and make positive changes to enhance their lives. Self-awareness also helps individuals to better understand and empathize with others, leading to improved communication and relationships.

There are generally two types of self-awareness: internal self-awareness and external self-awareness. Internal self-awareness is the ability to understand one's own values, beliefs, and emotions, while external self-awareness is the ability to understand how others perceive you.

Internal self-awareness[3] refers to a person's ability to introspect and understand their own thoughts, feelings, values, and beliefs. It involves self-reflection and self-examination to gain insight into one's own personality, emotions, and behaviors. Individuals who have a high degree of internal self-awareness are typically better able to understand their own motivations, preferences, and goals, and are more likely to make decisions that align with their values and interests.

External self-awareness[4], on the other hand, refers to a person's ability to perceive and understand how others see them. It involves being attuned to other people's perspectives and feedback and

---

[3] Ashley, Greg C., and Roni Reiter-Palmon. "Self-awareness and the evolution of leaders: The need for a better measure of self-awareness." *Journal of Behavioral and Applied Management* 14.1 (2012): 2-17.

[4] Eurich, Tasha. "What self-awareness really is (and how to cultivate it)." *Harvard Business Review* 4 (2018).

being able to accurately assess one's own behavior and impact on others. Individuals with high external self-awareness are typically better at reading social cues, understanding other people's emotions and perspectives, and building positive relationships with others. They are also more likely to be open to feedback and able to learn and grow from criticism.

Self-awareness can play an important role in improving our self-confidence. When we have a better understanding of our strengths, weaknesses, values, and beliefs, we are better equipped to navigate life's challenges and make decisions that align with our goals and values.

How Self-Awareness can improve Self-Confidence

Here are some ways self-awareness can help improve self-confidence:

Acknowledging and embracing strengths: Through self-awareness, we can identify and acknowledge our strengths, which can boost our confidence and sense of self-worth. By focusing on our abilities and successes, we can develop a positive self-image and feel more confident in our abilities.

Addressing and improving weaknesses: Self-awareness also involves recognizing our weaknesses or areas for improvement. By addressing these areas, we can work to improve ourselves and our skills, which can boost our confidence in our ability to grow and learn.

Building a positive self-image: By understanding how we see ourselves and how others see us (through feedback and open communication), we can work to build a positive self-image. A positive self-image can help us feel more confident and secure in who we are.

Setting and achieving goals: With self-awareness, we can set realistic and meaningful goals that align with our values and strengths. By achieving these goals, we can develop a sense of accomplishment and confidence in our abilities.

Overall, self-awareness can help us develop a more positive and realistic sense of self, which can lead to increased self-confidence and a greater sense of well-being.

The Johari Window[5] is an effective model that helps with the process of self-discovery and self-awareness. It consists of four quadrants that represent different aspects of our personality, known as the open, hidden, blind, and unknown areas.

THE JOHARI WINDOW

	KNOWN BY YOU	UNKNOWN BY YOU
KNOWN TO OTHERS	**OPEN** KNOWN BY BOTH YOU AND OTHERS	**BLIND SPOT** UNKNOWN TO YOU BUT KNOWN BY OTHERS
UNKNOWN TO OTHERS	**HIDDEN** KNOWN TO YOU BUT NOT BY OTHERS	**UNKNOWN** UNKNOWN BY BOTH YOU AND OTHERS

Positive examples of self-awareness through the Johari Window could include:

Open Area: This quadrant represents the information that is known to us and others. It includes our strengths, abilities, and personality traits that we are comfortable sharing with others. Positive examples of the open area could be a person who is aware of their

---

5 Saxena, Parul. "Johari Window: An effective model for improving interpersonal communication and managerial effectiveness." *SIT Journal of Management* 5.2 (2015): 134-146.

good communication skills and is comfortable expressing their emotions and needs to others.

Hidden Area: This quadrant represents the information that we know about ourselves, but others do not. It includes our private thoughts, feelings, and experiences. Positive examples of the hidden area could be a person who is aware of their creativity but doesn't share their art or writing with others yet.

Blind Area: This quadrant represents the information that others know about us, but we are not aware of. It includes our unconscious behaviors, biases, and assumptions. Positive examples of the blind area could be a person who is open to feedback from others and willing to learn about their blind spots to improve their relationships and communication.

Unknown Area: This quadrant represents the information that is unknown to both us and others. It includes our untapped potential, undiscovered talents, and unexplored experiences. Positive examples of the unknown area could be a person who is open to new experiences and is willing to explore their interests and passions to discover new talents and strengths.

In summary, the Johari Window can be a helpful tool for developing self-awareness and understanding our strengths, weaknesses, and potential. By focusing on positive examples, we can use this model to enhance our personal growth and relationships with others.

Being Valued as a Person

Being valued as a person is a fundamental human need that goes beyond basic physical and material requirements. It encompasses the emotional and psychological aspects of our being, providing us with a sense of purpose and meaning in life. It is the feeling of being seen, heard, and respected for who we are as individuals.

One of the most significant benefits of feeling valued is the boost it gives to our self-confidence and self-esteem. When we are recognized and appreciated for our contributions, we are more likely to feel good about ourselves and our abilities. This confidence, in turn, leads us to take on new challenges and pursue our goals with greater determination and resilience.

In contrast, feeling undervalued can have adverse effects on our mental and emotional health. When we feel ignored or invisible, it can lead to feelings of isolation, insecurity, and self-doubt. This can have a long-lasting impact on our sense of self-worth and confidence, making it harder for us to pursue our goals and live a fulfilling life.

To cultivate an environment that values individuals, it is crucial to actively listen and engage with others. This involves setting aside our biases and prejudices and approaching people with an open mind and heart. By doing so, we can better appreciate their unique perspectives and experiences, providing a sense of validation and recognition.

Expressing gratitude and appreciation for others is also essential. Whether it is a simple thank you or a more elaborate gesture, such as a thoughtful gift or kind words, acknowledging others' contributions can go a long way in making them feel valued and appreciated. This helps create a sense of connection and belonging, which is vital for our mental health and well-being.

Lastly, providing opportunities for individuals to showcase their unique talents and strengths can help build a culture of value and recognition. By doing so, we can create a sense of pride and accomplishment, boosting self-confidence and self-esteem.

In conclusion, being valued as a person is essential for our emotional and psychological well-being. It is about recognizing the inherent worth of every individual and providing them with a sense of belonging and purpose. By cultivating an environment of value and recognition, we can boost our self-confidence and the confidence of those around us, leading to a more fulfilling and satisfying life.

There are several ways in which we can improve our status in terms of being valued:

Cultivate self-worth: It is important to recognize and appreciate our own worth as individuals. We can do this by identifying our strengths, accomplishments, and unique qualities. By valuing ourselves, we can communicate our value to others.

Communicate our needs: It is important to communicate our needs to others in a clear and respectful manner. We can do this by expressing our opinions, asking for help when we need it, and setting boundaries when necessary.

Develop positive relationships: Positive relationships are key to feeling valued. We can build positive relationships by actively listening to others, showing empathy, and expressing appreciation and gratitude.

Recognize the value of others: It is important to recognize and appreciate the value of others. We can do this by actively listening, providing positive feedback, and showing appreciation for the contributions of others.

The World's Fastest Indian

The World's Fastest Indian[6] is a biographical drama film based on the true story of Burt Munro, an elderly motorcycle enthusiast from New Zealand who dreams of setting a land speed record at the Bonneville Salt Flats in Utah, USA. Munro prepares his motorcycle by making modifications to the engine and body and builds a special trailer to transport it to the race. Despite being faced with several obstacles, including financial struggles, health issues, and skeptical officials, Munro refuses to give up on his dream.

As he travels from New Zealand to the United States on his 1920 Indian motorcycle, Munro encounters numerous challenges. He struggles to raise the funds needed for the trip and faces visa issues, customs clearance difficulties, and mechanical problems with his motorcycle.

---

[6] Cox, Roger, dir. The World's Fastest Indian. Fox Searchlight Pictures, 2005.

Despite facing numerous obstacles and people who doubt and despise him, Munro refuses to give up on his dream of setting a land speed record on his modified Indian motorcycle. He faces skepticism and mockery from people who consider him too old and his motorcycle too outdated to achieve such a feat.

However, Munro remains undeterred and continues to work tirelessly on his motorcycle, even when faced with setbacks and financial difficulties. His unwavering self-belief is contagious, and he eventually wins over some of his detractors, including a skeptical official who initially denies him the chance to compete at the Bonneville Salt Flats.

Munro's character in the film embodies the importance of believing in oneself and having self-confidence, even in the face of doubt and adversity. His determination and positive attitude inspire others to believe in him, ultimately leading to his success in setting a new land speed record. Munro's self-confidence is further evident in the way he presents himself to others. He remains polite, respectful, and unassuming, but never lets anyone else's doubts or negativity affect his mindset. His determination and positive attitude inspire others to believe in him, and ultimately lead to his achieving his dream.

The Straight Story

The Straight Story[7] is a film about second chances, self-confidence, and perseverance. The film follows Alvin Straight, a elderly man who lives in Iowa and has recently suffered a stroke. Alvin is determined to reconnect with his estranged brother Lyle, who lives in Wisconsin and whom he hasn't seen in years. However, Alvin's health is too poor to drive, so he decides to make the trip on his riding lawnmower.

Throughout his journey, Alvin faces many challenges, including mechanical issues with his lawnmower and health setbacks. Despite these obstacles, Alvin remains determined to reach his brother and

---

[7] Lynch, David, dir. The Straight Story. Buena Vista Pictures Distribution, 1999.

make amends. He meets many people along the way, including a runaway teenage girl, a sympathetic priest, and a group of bikers, who all help him in their own ways.

Alvin's self-confidence and perseverance are evident in the way he handles these challenges. He doesn't let setbacks discourage him, and he always finds a way to keep moving forward. For example, when his lawnmower breaks down, he doesn't quit and find a solution to fix it, despite his age and health issues. His resourcefulness and determination are admirable, and they inspire those around him.

Moreover, the film highlights the theme of second chances, as Alvin tries to reconcile with his brother Lyle. Despite their past conflicts, Alvin is determined to make amends and seek forgiveness. Through his journey, he realizes the importance of family and forgiveness, and the power of second chances. This serves as a reminder to the audience that it's never too late to seek forgiveness or start over.

In conclusion, The Straight Story is a film that celebrates second chances, self-confidence, and perseverance. Through Alvin's journey, we see the power of determination and the importance of family and forgiveness. The film reminds us that no matter how old we are or how difficult the journey may be, we should always have the courage to keep moving forward and never give up on our goals.

The Lessons from Two Movies

The common lessons from The World's Fastest Indian and The Straight Story are the importance of self-belief, determination, and perseverance. Both films feature elderly protagonists who face significant obstacles, but refuse to give up on their dreams. Despite being faced with adversity, they remain determined to achieve their goals, and their positive attitudes inspire those around them to believe in them as well.

In both films, the protagonists face challenges that test their physical and emotional strength, yet they maintain their self-confidence and never lose sight of their goals. The films emphasize the importance of believing in oneself, and the power of positive thinking in the face of adversity. Furthermore, both films show that one is never too old to pursue their dreams or seek forgiveness and make amends.

The protagonists of both films also highlight the theme of second chances, as they try to reconcile with past conflicts and seek forgiveness. The films encourage the audience to reflect on their own lives and relationships, and to always have the courage to start anew and pursue their goals.

In summary, both The World's Fastest Indian and The Straight Story emphasize the importance of self-confidence, determination, perseverance, and second chances. They celebrate the human spirit and the power of positive thinking, inspiring the audience to never give up on their dreams, no matter how difficult the journey may be.

Chapter Summary:

This chapter explores the concept of self-awareness, its types, and the ways to increase one's value through it. Self-awareness is defined as the ability to introspect and comprehend our thoughts, feelings, and behaviors. It plays a critical role in recognizing our strengths and weaknesses, shaping our actions, and interacting with others. It is instrumental in personal growth, development, and fostering relationships.

Self-awareness has two primary types: internal and external. Internal self-awareness involves understanding our own emotions, values, and beliefs through self-reflection. It aids in comprehending our motivations, preferences, and goals, thereby enabling us to make decisions in line with our values and interests. External self-awareness, on the contrary, deals with perceiving how others see us. It is about interpreting social cues, understanding others' emotions and perspectives, and forming positive relationships. Those with high external self-awareness tend to be receptive to feedback, learning from criticism, and making improvements.

Chapter Lessons

1. Self-awareness is pivotal for personal growth and development, helping us understand our strengths, weaknesses, motivations, and goals.
2. Internal self-awareness involves introspection, enabling us to align our decisions with our values and interests. External self-awareness involves understanding how we are perceived by others, which helps build positive relationships and grow from criticism.
3. Self-value can be enhanced by cultivating self-worth, communicating our needs effectively, developing positive relationships, and recognizing the value in others.
4. Self-awareness plays a crucial role in improving self-confidence, better decision-making, and effectively handling life's challenges.

Chapter 3 Developing Self-Confidence

Self-confidence plays a significant role in our willingness to take a second chance. When we lack confidence in ourselves, we may be hesitant to try again after a failure or setback, fearing that we will fail again. On the other hand, when we have self-confidence, we are more likely to view setbacks as temporary and believe that we have the ability to succeed in the future.

Self-confidence allows us to approach second chances with a positive attitude and a growth mindset. It enables us to reflect on our mistakes and learn from them, rather than dwelling on them and feeling defeated. When we have self-confidence, we are more likely to take responsibility for our actions and look for solutions to overcome challenges.

In contrast, low self-confidence can cause us to avoid second chances altogether, leading us to miss out on opportunities for growth and success. We may doubt our abilities and feel unworthy of a second chance, leading us to give up without trying again.

Therefore, developing self-confidence is crucial for embracing second chances and achieving our goals. By believing in ourselves and our ability to learn and grow from our mistakes, we can approach second chances with a positive mindset and a determination to succeed.

Self-Confidence

Confidence is a critical ingredient in life. It is the key that unlocks the door to utilizing our abilities and knowledge. Without it, even simple tasks can feel overwhelming, and the thought of speaking in public or asking a question can be terrifying. The absence of self-assurance can lead to a sense of inadequacy, which can impact our personal and professional lives in countless ways.

For instance, when attending a seminar, the lack of confidence can prevent us from actively participating, which can hinder our ability to learn and grow. Even during a job interview, nerves can take over, causing us to stumble over our words, break into a sweat, and perform poorly. Low self-esteem can also make it challenging to communicate with someone of the opposite sex or form healthy relationships with peers of the same gender.

On the other hand, when we possess a healthy dose of self-belief, we become empowered to move, act, socialize, and chase our dreams. Confidence is the spark that ignites the flame, leading to a fulfilling and meaningful existence. When we have faith in ourselves, we become more resilient and better equipped to deal with challenges and obstacles.

Confidence also breeds success. It attracts people to us and opens up opportunities we may have never imagined. It enables us to pursue our passions and take calculated risks that lead to personal and professional growth. In turn, this boosts our self-esteem and reinforces our belief in ourselves, creating a cycle of positivity and achievement.

To cultivate self-confidence, we must learn to recognize and challenge our negative self-talk, replace it with positive affirmations, and embrace our strengths and weaknesses. We should also surround ourselves with supportive people who encourage us to step out of our comfort zones and believe in our potential.

In conclusion, self-confidence is the foundation of our existence. It allows us to unlock our full potential and live a fulfilling and meaningful life. With confidence, we become empowered to take on challenges, pursue our passions, and achieve our dreams. Therefore, it is vital to cultivate and nurture our confidence and use it as a tool to enhance our personal and professional lives.

Development of Self-Confidence

Self-confidence is a crucial aspect of personal development. It is something that evolves over time and can be divided into two periods:
- Development of Self-Confidence During Childhood and Adolescence
- Development of Self-Confidence During Adulthood

Development of Self-Confidence During Childhood and Adolescence

The first period is childhood and adolescence, which lasts until the individual reaches 18 years old and becomes an adult. During this time, self-confidence can be heavily influenced by external factors such as family, peers, and experiences. Children who grow up in a supportive and encouraging environment are more likely to develop a healthy sense of self-esteem and self-worth. However, negative experiences, such as bullying or rejection, can significantly impact a child's confidence and self-belief.

Self-confidence is the foundation of personal growth and success, and it starts with the belief that we can achieve our goals. Unfortunately, from a young age, many of us are told what we can't do instead of what we can. Expressions such as "children should be seen and not heard" or belittling comments from parents, uncles, grandparents, and other elders can damage our self-esteem and hinder the development of self-confidence.

The development of self-confidence is largely influenced by parents or caregivers. When parents are overly protective and systematically solve their children's problems, such as providing private lessons without the child's request, they inadvertently inhibit the development of their child's self-confidence.

Additionally, children whose balance of criticism and love is disrupted, either being excessively criticized or excessively loved without receiving necessary criticism, are more likely to experience self-confidence issues in adulthood.

Especially children who have been subjected to a lot of negative criticism from their elders, regardless of their talents and intelligence, are more likely to struggle with expressing themselves, taking risks, and making decisions as adults.

It's important for parents and caregivers to provide a supportive and encouraging environment that fosters self-confidence in children. This includes offering constructive feedback, allowing them to make mistakes and learn from them, and recognizing and celebrating their strengths and accomplishments.

Development of Self-Confidence During Adulthood

The second period is adulthood, which spans throughout the rest of an individual's life. In this stage, self-confidence can continue to be influenced by external factors, but it also becomes more reliant on internal factors such as personal achievements and self-reflection. People who have developed a healthy level of self-confidence in their childhood and adolescence are more likely to continue to grow and thrive in adulthood. However, individuals who have struggled with confidence issues in their earlier years can still work on developing their self-esteem through various means such as therapy, positive self-talk, and taking risks.

During adulthood, an individual's self-confidence can be influenced by both external and internal factors. External factors might include their relationships, job, or experiences, whereas internal factors are more personal and include factors such as their self-image, self-talk, and self-worth.

For example, if someone has a positive self-image and believes in their abilities, they are more likely to take on challenges and try new things, leading to increased self-confidence. Conversely, if someone has a negative self-image, they may feel inadequate and struggle to take risks or try new things, leading to decreased self-confidence.

People who have developed a healthy level of self-confidence in their childhood and adolescence are more likely to continue to grow and thrive in adulthood. For instance, someone who grew up in an environment where they were encouraged to take risks and believe in themselves may have a more positive self-image as an adult and be more willing to try new things and take on challenges.

However, individuals who have struggled with confidence issues in their earlier years can still work on developing their self-esteem in adulthood. This might involve seeking therapy to address past trauma or negative experiences, practicing positive self-talk to reframe negative thoughts, and taking calculated risks to build confidence in their abilities.

For example, if someone struggles with social anxiety and lacks confidence in social situations, they might seek therapy to address the root causes of their anxiety and develop coping strategies. They might also practice positive self-talk, such as telling themselves that they are capable of making new friends or engaging in social activities. Taking small steps, such as attending a social event or reaching out to someone new, can also help build their confidence over time.

In conclusion, self-confidence is a complex and dynamic concept that can be influenced by a range of internal and external factors. While childhood experiences can set the foundation for self-confidence, it is possible to develop and improve self-esteem throughout adulthood through various means such as therapy, positive self-talk, and taking risks

In conclusion, the development of self-confidence is a continuous process that spans throughout our lifetime. The childhood and adolescence period set the foundation for self-confidence, while adulthood offers opportunities for growth and development. Regardless of our past experiences, we can work towards building a healthy level of self-confidence by investing in ourselves, surrounding ourselves with positivity, and learning to celebrate our achievements.

Self-Confidence as a Journey

Developing self-confidence is a journey that requires patience and persistence. It involves pushing oneself out of the comfort zone and taking on challenges that may seem daunting at first. However, with each small step, self-confidence can grow and flourish.

One effective way to develop self-confidence is through setting achievable goals and gradually increasing their difficulty. This could be as simple as striking up a conversation with a stranger, taking on a new hobby, or signing up for a class. By taking action and achieving these goals, individuals can build their confidence and prove to themselves that they are capable of achieving success.

There are various ways to improve self-confidence and one of them is by engaging in small projects or activities. For instance, you can choose to beautify your room by decorating a section of it based on a theme, such as musical instruments. By doing so, you can ask yourself questions like which musical instruments would fit the theme and how you can find and purchase them economically. This would require you to communicate with others, such as music instrument sellers, antique shops, or music schools, which can also help you express yourself better.

Moreover, it's important to recognize that being a good speaker is not an innate talent, but a skill that can be learned through practice. Similarly, people who lack innate talent in a particular area can still develop various skills through training. For example, training in areas such as sales and painting can help individuals develop their skills and, in turn, improve their self-confidence. As they become more skilled and confident in these areas, they may feel more comfortable taking on new challenges and pursuing their goals.

The founder of Modern Turkey, Ataturk, had a powerful message for the Turkish people with his call, "Turk, be proud, work, trust." This message holds true for personal development as well. Expanding on his quote, we can interpret it as follows: "Turk, be proud and believe in your abilities to accomplish your goals; work hard and take action to achieve those goals; trust in yourself and your ability to succeed by seeing the results of your efforts."

Three Levels of Self-Confidence
Self-confidence can be categorized into three types:
- *those with low or no self-confidence,*
- *those with average self-confidence,*
- *and those with very high self-confidence.*

But what causes low self-confidence? We all start out equal in life, with some having innate talents, but self-confidence is a trait that is learned or lost over time. Babies and children are naturally curious and eager to explore their surroundings, but some are freer to do so from the age of one than others. The reason for this difference lies in the behavior of those who raise the child, not the child itself.

Let's consider three children who are all average intelligence and are ordinary in every way.

The first child is constantly criticized, with their mistakes constantly emphasized and addressed with negative words. They are told to sit still and not move.

The second child is criticized for most of their actions, and their movements are restricted.

The third child is treated differently, with their incorrect behavior kindly pointed out and praised in a positive manner. They are encouraged to try new things and frequently addressed with positive words.

As these three children grow up, the first child struggles in school, has difficulty making friends, expressing themselves, and communicating with the opposite sex. They also struggle to learn and fail college and university entrance exams.

The second child achieves average success in school, but they are not socially enterprising and fail college entrance exams, only passing university entrance exams.

The third child is very successful in some school subjects and successful in most others, popular among peers and socially enterprising. They are willing to take on tasks, have both small and large successes, and believe they will pass college and university entrance exams, which they do.

At first glance, you might think that these three children, who started off equal, are no longer equal. However, they maintain their equality in terms of capacity. The differences in their self-confidence stem from the behavior of others towards them. Negative words and behaviors do not diminish us; just like no matter how much you curse or hit a 100 dollar bill, it will maintain its value.

Therefore, the main issue for people with low self-confidence is not the inability to trust themselves but the belief that they cannot trust themselves. Changing this belief themselves can solve the problem, but if they cannot, they can adopt the formula of the third child with high self-confidence.

The third child's self-confidence has increased due to their success in small and large projects and gaining experience. Success in small projects encourages them to start larger projects. Additionally, these successes render the opinions of people in our surroundings insignificant or transform their opinions into positive ones.

Regardless of age or level of self-confidence, daring to try a trial within one's current level of self-confidence and succeeding will increase self-confidence.

Vicious Cycle and Self-Confidence

Individuals often make broad statements about themselves, with some seeing themselves as confident while others claiming to have no self-confidence whatsoever. However, these views are often oversimplified.

Everyone possesses self-confidence in certain areas. For example, a mom may be nervous about public speaking but might be an excellent cook, leading to confidence in this domain. Similarly, a student may struggle with math but excel at computer games. A professional may lack confidence in making a presentation or but feel competent in skiing. Thus, it is unreasonable to conclude that someone's self-confidence is either high or low. Rather, it is reasonable to assume that individuals have high confidence in areas where they perceive themselves as successful and low confidence in areas where they struggle.

Many people tend to evaluate their self-confidence as generally high or low, even though confidence relates to specific skills or performance areas. This approach is influenced by the areas they focus on when assessing themselves. If someone evaluates themselves based on their weaknesses, they may perceive themselves as having low self-confidence. Therefore, it is beneficial to concentrate on one's strengths to improve overall self-confidence.

High self-confidence enables people to succeed in new ventures and persist despite setbacks. People who have been praised and recognized for their positive traits since childhood and have positive beliefs about themselves face similar challenges to others in their endeavors. Conversely, individuals with low self-confidence encounter similar problems but tend to overcome obstacles more slowly than their high self-confidence counterparts.

A person with high self-confidence finds learning a new skill more manageable, while those with low self-confidence may struggle. This creates a vicious cycle of positive and negative thinking, where individuals with high self-confidence approach situations confidently and succeed, increasing their self-confidence even further. On the other hand, people with low self-confidence tend to think negatively, leading to failure and decreasing confidence.

People have an optimistic and a pessimistic "angel" on their shoulders, with the former encouraging positive behavior and the latter criticizing and predicting failure. Those with high self-confidence listen to their optimistic angel, while those with low self-confidence often listen to the pessimistic one.

In conclusion, focusing on one's strengths is an effective way to boost overall self-confidence. Negative thinking does not guarantee maintaining the status quo, and excessive negative thinking can worsen the situation. Positive and rational negative thinking can help individuals take appropriate precautions to overcome obstacles.

The Story of The Kid

The Kid[8] is a science fiction movie starring Bruce Willis, where he plays an old man named Russ Duritz, a successful but lonely image consultant. One day, he meets a young boy named Rusty, who is actually himself as a child. Russ is shocked to see his younger self and begins to question the choices he has made in life.

As Rusty spends time with Russ, he helps him confront his past and rediscover his true self. Through their interactions, Russ begins to regain his lost self-confidence and sense of worth. Rusty helps Russ realize that he has been living his life based on the expectations of others, rather than his own desires and values.

---

[8] Turteltaub, Jon, dir. The Kid. Touchstone Pictures, 2000.

Through their conversations and experiences together, Russ begins to understand the importance of being true to oneself and following one's own dreams, rather than constantly seeking external validation and approval. With Rusty's help, Russ learns to let go of his past regrets and focus on the present moment, finding joy and fulfillment in life once again.

As the story progresses, Russ also learns the value of relationships and being valued as a person. Through his interactions with Rusty, he realizes that he has been neglecting the people who truly matter in his life. He begins to rebuild his relationships with his family and friends, recognizing their importance in his life and valuing them for who they are.

In the end, The Kid is a heartwarming story of self-discovery, self-confidence, and being valued for who you are as a person. Russ's journey towards rediscovering his true self and rekindling his relationships serves as a reminder of the importance of staying true to oneself and valuing the people who matter in our lives.

The Story of Shall We Dance

Shall We Dance[9] is a romantic comedy-drama that follows the life of John Clark (Richard Gere), a successful lawyer who is struggling to find fulfillment and happiness in his daily routine. One evening, while riding the train home from work, John glimpses a beautiful woman (Jennifer Lopez) in the window of Miss Mitzi's Dance Studio. Intrigued, he decides to follow his curiosity and impulsively signs up for ballroom dancing lessons.

At first, John struggles to break out of his mundane routine and feel comfortable with dancing. He keeps his lessons a secret from his wife, Beverly (Susan Sarandon), and tries to maintain a normal life while pursuing his newfound passion. Along the way, he develops a friendship with his dance instructor, Paulina (Jennifer Lopez), who encourages him to keep going and helps him find his inner rhythm.

---

[9] Chelsom, Peter, dir. Shall We Dance. Miramax Films, 2004.

As John becomes more involved in the world of ballroom dancing, he discovers a sense of joy and excitement that he had been missing in his life. He learns new skills, gains confidence, and forms meaningful connections with the people around him. However, his secret lessons eventually strain his relationship with his wife, who suspects that he is having an affair.

Ultimately, John realizes that he cannot keep his passion for dancing hidden and comes clean to Beverly. In a heartwarming scene, they attend a ballroom dance competition together and rekindle their love for each other. John's decision to break out of his routine, learn new skills, and pursue his passion for dancing ultimately leads to a second chance in his relationship and a renewed sense of purpose in his life.

In conclusion, Shall We Dance is a film that celebrates the importance of breaking routines, learning new skills, and creating second chances. John's journey serves as a reminder that it is never too late to pursue your passions and find fulfillment in life. Through his love for ballroom dancing, John gains self-confidence, breaks out of his mundane routine, and forms meaningful connections with the people around him. Ultimately, his decision to take a chance on something new leads to a happier, more fulfilling life.

Chapter Summary

- Developing self-confidence is a journey that requires patience, persistence, and stepping outside of your comfort zone.
- Setting achievable goals and gradually increasing their difficulty can boost confidence.
- Engaging in small projects and activities is another effective method for self-confidence improvement.
- Being a good speaker or excelling in a certain skill isn't necessarily an innate talent but can be learned through practice.
- Self-confidence can be categorized into three types: low or no self-confidence, average self-confidence, and very high self-confidence. The differences in these levels often stem from childhood experiences.

- Evaluations of self-confidence should not be generalized but recognized in relation to specific skills or areas.
- Focusing on one's strengths can improve overall self-confidence and enable people to succeed in new ventures and persist despite setbacks.
- A vicious cycle exists between positive and negative thinking and self-confidence levels.

Chapter Lessons

- Persistence and pushing one's boundaries are vital in the journey of developing self-confidence.
- Small, achievable goals can lead to greater confidence over time. Starting with smaller projects can also serve as an effective way to build self-confidence.
- Everyone possesses self-confidence in certain areas. Identifying and focusing on these strengths can lead to an overall boost in self-confidence.
- Negative or pessimistic thinking can be detrimental to self-confidence. Thus, it's essential to foster positive thinking and rational negative thinking to help overcome obstacles.
- Self-confidence levels often trace back to the behavior of caregivers during childhood. Changing beliefs about one's own capabilities can drastically improve self-confidence.
- Everyone possesses both optimistic and pessimistic "angels". Listening to the optimistic one and silencing the pessimistic one can lead to a better self-image and heightened self-confidence.

If We Want...

Let's finish this chapter with a poem. The inspiration to this poem is another poem written in Turkish by Dr. Ömer Kaplan, Biz İstersek- If we want.

If we want, mountains can crumble into dust,
Iron can transform, and swords into rust.
With open hearts and spirits strong,
We can harness our powers and right every wrong.
With love, we turn darkness into light,
Make present memories shining so bright,

And create life as a grand symphony,
Filled with sweet melodies and harmony.
We fight for our beliefs, with honor and pride,
Time bends to our will, and we never hide.
Our self-confidence defines us, no need to discuss,
There is no winter, for us, it's always spring to us.

Chapter 4 Overcoming and Confronting Trauma

The concept of ghosts varies widely across different cultures and belief systems, so there is no one definitive answer to this question. However, in general, ghosts[10] are believed to be the spirits of dead people who have not yet moved on to the afterlife or have some unfinished business in the world of the living.

In many cultures, ghosts are believed to be able to interact with the physical world in various ways, such as moving objects, making noises, or even appearing as apparitions. Some people believe that ghosts may have specific functions, such as seeking revenge, delivering messages, or guiding the living.

In some belief systems, ghosts may be thought of as being stuck in a state of limbo, unable to move on to the afterlife until they have fulfilled certain obligations or resolved certain issues. This could include unfinished business, unresolved conflicts, or the need to pass on important information or knowledge to the living.

Ghosts and traumas can be similar in a few ways.

Firstly, both traumas and ghosts can be invisible yet powerful forces that affect our lives. Traumas can leave lasting emotional scars and impact our behavior and relationships, while ghosts are believed to be spirits that linger in the physical world and can influence people and events.

Secondly, both traumas and ghosts can be difficult to confront and process. Traumas can be painful and overwhelming, and may require therapy or other forms of support to address. Similarly, ghosts can be unsettling and frightening, and may require the help of a spiritual practitioner or medium to resolve.

Lastly, both traumas and fictitious ghosts can have a lingering presence in our lives, even after we think we have moved on. Traumas can resurface unexpectedly and continue to impact us, while ghosts may return or remain in a location long after their initial appearance or presence.

---

[10] Bell, Michael Mayerfeld. "The ghosts of place." Theory and society 26.6 (1997): 813-836.

Overall, while traumas and ghosts may be different in their nature and origin, they share some similarities in the ways they can impact and linger in our lives.

Obstacles in Seizing Our Second Chances

Creating and seizing second chances often involve navigating through a multitude of challenges. Among these, unresolved traumas can pose significant obstacles, preventing individuals from moving forward.

Traumas, resulting from distressing experiences or events, can leave lasting emotional imprints that subtly guide our actions and decisions. These invisible yet powerful influences can unconsciously shape our behavior, steering us away from perceived threats or discomfort. This limiting effect reduces our willingness to take risks, explore new experiences, or seize second chances. Confronting and processing traumas can be an intimidating task. The intensity of the pain and overwhelm caused by traumas can be paralyzing, making the path towards resolution feel steep and arduous. This fear and avoidance of addressing traumas directly impede our ability to embrace new possibilities. Until we can confront and process these traumas, they can obstruct our progress, keeping us anchored to our pasts and inhibiting our movement towards the future.

Moreover, the lingering presence of unresolved traumas can disrupt our lives unexpectedly and potentially derail our second chances. Even when we believe we've moved on, these traumas can reemerge, triggered by certain events, experiences, or reminders. These unexpected resurgences can create emotional turmoil and hinder our ability to fully engage with new opportunities or changes.

Unresolved traumas can pose substantial obstacles in creating and utilizing second chances. These traumas can trap individuals in their pasts, impede their present, and limit their futures. To truly seize second chances, we must confront and process these traumas, allowing us to move beyond our pasts and fully embrace new possibilities.

The Courage to Purr: Rosemary's Journey from Fear to Confidence

Rosemary was a woman in her forties who had always been terrified of cats. As a child, she had a traumatic experience with a stray cat that had scratched her hand, leaving a deep wound that required stitches. Ever since that day, the mere sight of a cat would make her heart race and her palms sweat.

Despite her fear, Rosemary had managed to avoid cats for most of her life. She lived in a cat-free home and avoided places where cats were likely to be found. However, this all changed when she started dating a man named Tom, who happened to be a cat lover.

At first, Rosemary tried to keep her fear hidden from Tom, but eventually, she had to confess her phobia to him. To her surprise, Tom was very understanding and offered to help her overcome her fear.

He started by introducing her to his own cat, a friendly tabby named Whiskers. At first, Rosemary was hesitant to even be in the same room as the cat, but over time, she began to feel more comfortable. Tom taught her how to interact with the cat and how to read its body language to avoid triggering any fearful responses.

Eventually, Rosemary was able to spend time around cats without feeling anxious or scared. Tom even took her to a cat cafe where she was able to enjoy the company of many different cats. She even found herself petting them and enjoying their company.

Overcoming her fear of cats had a profound impact on Rosemary. She felt more confident in herself and her ability to face her fears. She realized that sometimes, facing our fears head-on is the best way to overcome them. And with Tom by her side, she was able to do just that.

Driving Each Other Crazy: A Tale of Trust and Anxiety

Johan and his wife, Maria, have been married for over a decade. They have always had a close relationship and have been through many ups and downs together. However, one thing that has always been a point of contention between them is Maria's driving.

Johan is an extremely cautious person, and this carries over to his approach to driving. He always insists on following the speed limit, using turn signals, and checking his mirrors frequently. He also has a habit of warning Maria whenever she is behind the wheel, which has become a point of frustration for both of them.

Despite this, Maria is a confident driver and has never been in a serious accident. She resents Johan's constant warnings and feels that he does not trust her abilities. However, Johan cannot shake his fear of something happening while Maria is driving, and he worries constantly about her safety.

One day, while they are driving home from a family gathering, Johan's fears come to life. Maria takes a corner too quickly and loses control of the car, skidding off the road and into a ditch. Johan is shaken but unhurt, but Maria suffers a broken arm and a concussion.

As they recover from the accident, Johan realizes that his constant warnings and fear may have contributed to the accident. He apologizes to Maria for not trusting her abilities and promises to work on his anxieties. Maria forgives him, and they work together to overcome their fears and anxieties surrounding driving.

In the end, the accident serves as a wake-up call for both of them, and they learn to trust each other and communicate better on the road. Johan still worries, but he has learned to express his concerns in a more constructive way, and Maria has learned to listen to his feedback without feeling judged or belittled.

The Art of Mindful Dating: Alexandra's Lessons in Finding True Love

Alexandra had been married for 10 years before she got divorced. After a few years of living alone, she began to feel the need for companionship and wanted to remarry. However, every man who proposed to her seemed to have some sort of problem, and she found it difficult to establish a healthy relationship.

One man was too controlling, another was too distant, and yet another was too clingy. Alexandra found herself getting frustrated and losing hope of ever finding someone who was right for her. She began to wonder if there was something wrong with her that was keeping her from finding a good partner.

Despite her frustration, Alexandra refused to give up on her dream of finding love again. She began to reflect on her previous relationships and realized that she had been ignoring some important red flags. She had been so eager to be in a relationship that she had overlooked some of the warning signs that her partners were not a good match for her.

With this realization, Alexandra began to focus on developing her self-awareness and being more mindful of the qualities she was looking for in a partner. She also sought the help of a therapist who helped her work through her past traumas and insecurities.

As she continued to work on herself, Alexandra met a man who seemed to have all the qualities she was looking for. He was kind, supportive, and had a great sense of humor. Despite her fears and doubts, Alexandra decided to take a chance and enter into a relationship with him.

At first, it was difficult for her to trust him completely and she found herself getting anxious and defensive at times. But with time and patience, she learned to open up and be vulnerable with him. As they grew closer, Alexandra realized that she had finally found someone who valued her for who she was and treated her with the love and respect she deserved.

In conclusion, Alexandra's journey to finding love again was not easy, but it was a journey of self-discovery and growth. By being more mindful of her own needs and learning to trust herself, she was able to establish a healthy relationship with a man who appreciated her for who she was.

The Machinist

The movie "The Machinist" directed by Brad Anderson portrays the theme of how past traumas can have a lingering presence in our lives, even after we think we have moved on. Throughout the film, the main character Trevor Reznik experiences the consequences of a traumatic event and its subsequent impact on his mental state and behavior.

Trevor's past trauma is revealed to be the hit-and-run incident involving a boy, which he repressed in his memory. The guilt from this accident becomes the root cause of his insomnia, emaciation, and overall deteriorating mental and physical health. His appearance and behavior isolate him from his coworkers, and the accident at work, where his coworker loses his arm, exacerbates the animosity towards him.

The film portrays how Trevor's traumatic experience resurfaces unexpectedly, manifesting as hallucinations and a series of bizarre events. He becomes increasingly paranoid, feeling targeted by a mysterious presence. The recurring imagery, such as the menacing cigarette lighter and the post-it notes depicting a hangman game, further contribute to his deteriorating mental state.

Trevor's attempts to establish connections with Stevie, a prostitute, and Maria, a waitress, represent his longing for comfort and companionship. However, even in these relationships, the traumas of his past haunt him, and he becomes suspicious of those around him. His paranoia leads him to accuse Stevie of conspiring against him, and he discovers that Maria doesn't actually exist.

The twist in the plot reveals that Trevor's perception of Ivan, an unfamiliar coworker, was a figment of his imagination. Ivan represents Trevor's guilt and serves as a manifestation of the hit-

and-run incident. Trevor's confrontation with Ivan, his failed attempt to dispose of his body, and the revelation that Ivan is unharmed solidify the notion that Ivan was never real but rather a projection of Trevor's guilty conscience.

In the end, Trevor's realization of his past actions and his decision to confess at the police station represent his acknowledgment of the trauma he caused and his acceptance of responsibility. By confessing and seeking closure, Trevor takes the first step towards confronting his trauma and potentially finding a path towards healing.

"The Machinist" effectively portrays how past traumas can resurface unexpectedly and continue to impact an individual's life, leading to paranoia, guilt, and a distorted perception of reality. Trevor's journey exemplifies the profound and lasting effects of trauma on an individual's mental and emotional well-being, illustrating the importance of acknowledging and addressing past traumas for healing and growth.

The Five Methods to Overcome Trauma
1. Talking Therapy

Talking therapy, also known as psychotherapy[11] or counseling, is a therapeutic approach that involves talking with a trained mental health professional, such as a psychologist or therapist. It is designed to provide a supportive and non-judgmental environment for individuals to explore and process their traumatic experiences.

In talking therapy, the therapist creates a safe space where you can freely express your thoughts, emotions, and reactions related to the trauma. The therapist listens attentively and helps you delve into the details of your experiences, allowing you to gain a deeper understanding of what happened and how it has affected you.

One of the primary goals of talking therapy is to help you manage the thoughts and emotions that arise from the trauma. The therapist

---

[11] Lambert, Michael J., Allen E. Bergin, and S. L. Garfield. "The effectiveness of psychotherapy." *Encyclopedia of psychotherapy* 1 (1994): 709-714.

assists you in identifying and challenging any negative beliefs or distorted thinking patterns that may have developed as a result of the trauma. By examining these thoughts and beliefs, you can learn to replace them with more balanced and accurate perspectives.

Additionally, the therapist provides guidance and teaches you specific skills and techniques to cope with the impact of trauma. This may involve learning relaxation techniques to manage stress and anxiety, developing healthy coping strategies to deal with triggers or flashbacks, and practicing self-care and self-compassion.

Talking therapy is a collaborative process where you work together with the therapist to address your unique needs and goals. The therapist provides support, validation, and guidance throughout the therapeutic journey, helping you navigate the healing process and develop resilience in the face of trauma.

It's important to note that the specific approach and techniques used in talking therapy can vary depending on the therapist's training and the individual's needs. Some common types of talking therapy for trauma include Trauma-focused Cognitive Behavioral Therapy (TF-CBT), Psychodynamic Therapy, and Narrative Therapy. The choice of therapy will depend on factors such as the nature of the trauma, individual preferences, and the therapist's expertise.

2. *Facing Your Fears Therapy*

Facing Your Fears therapy, also known as exposure therapy[12], is a type of cognitive-behavioral therapy that aims to reduce the distress and avoidance behaviors associated with traumatic memories or situations. It involves gradually exposing yourself to the memories or triggers related to the trauma in a safe and controlled manner. The therapy begins by collaboratively identifying specific situations, objects, or memories that evoke fear or distress. These can be directly related to the traumatic event or reminders that trigger anxiety and avoidance behaviors. Together with a therapist, you

---

[12] Richard, David CS, and Dean Lauterbach, eds. Handbook of exposure therapies. Elsevier, 2011.

create a hierarchy or a list of these fear-inducing items, arranging them from least distressing to most distressing.
Starting with the least distressing item, you expose yourself to it in a safe and controlled environment. This may involve mentally visualizing the memory or confronting the trigger directly in a real-life situation. The therapist provides support, guidance, and techniques to help you manage the resulting distress, such as relaxation exercises or cognitive restructuring.

As you become more comfortable and less anxious with each exposure, you gradually move up the hierarchy to face more distressing situations or memories. The goal is to desensitize your response to the fear-inducing stimuli, allowing you to develop new associations and reduce the distress associated with the traumatic memories or triggers.

By confronting your fears in a supportive environment, you have the opportunity to learn that the feared outcomes or overwhelming emotions you associate with the trauma are not as threatening as you initially believed. This can help challenge and modify negative beliefs and perceptions associated with the traumatic event. Through repeated exposure, you can also develop new coping skills and adaptive behaviors to manage distress. The therapy aims to break the cycle of avoidance, as avoidance behaviors tend to maintain and intensify anxiety and prevent natural recovery.

3. *Changing Negative Thoughts therapy*

Changing Negative Thoughts therapy, often based on cognitive-behavioral therapy (CBT)[13] principles, involves identifying and challenging negative beliefs and thoughts associated with the trauma. The goal is to modify unhelpful thinking patterns and replace them with more positive, realistic, and adaptive thoughts. In this therapy, you work collaboratively with a therapist to become aware of the negative thoughts and beliefs that arise in relation to the trauma. These thoughts often contribute to distress, self-blame, guilt, or a sense of helplessness.

---

[13] Turner, Rhonda, and Susan M. Swearer Napolitano. "Cognitive behavioral therapy (CBT)." (2010).

The therapist helps you identify and examine these negative thoughts, often referred to as cognitive distortions, which are inaccurate or unhelpful interpretations of the traumatic event or its consequences. Some common cognitive distortions include catastrophizing (exaggerating the negative impact), personalization (attributing excessive blame to oneself), or overgeneralization (drawing broad negative conclusions based on a single event). Once these negative thoughts are identified, the therapist guides you in challenging their accuracy and rationality. You learn to question the evidence and validity of these thoughts, considering alternative explanations or perspectives. This process helps to break the cycle of negative thinking and encourages more balanced and realistic thoughts to emerge.

Through therapy, you develop strategies and techniques to replace negative thoughts with more positive and adaptive ones. This may involve reframing the traumatic event, finding alternative explanations, or focusing on strengths and resilience. The therapist may provide cognitive restructuring exercises or homework assignments to practice identifying and challenging negative thoughts outside of therapy sessions.
By actively working to change negative thoughts, you can reshape your perception of the trauma and its effects on your life. This process can lead to a reduction in distress, self-blame, and feelings of helplessness. It empowers you to gain a more balanced perspective, fostering a sense of control and promoting emotional healing.

4. *Mindfulness and Relaxation approaches*

Mindfulness and Relaxation[14] approaches involve practicing techniques that cultivate a state of present-moment awareness and relaxation. These practices can be beneficial in the context of trauma by helping you develop a calmer and more compassionate perspective on your traumatic experiences. Here's a closer look at this therapeutic approach:

---

[14] Smith, Jonathan C.. Relaxation, Meditation, & Mindfulness: A Mental Health Practitioner's Guide to New and Traditional Approaches. Ukrayna, Springer Publishing Company, 2005.

- *Mindfulness:* Mindfulness involves intentionally paying attention to the present moment with an attitude of non-judgmental awareness. Through mindfulness practices, such as meditation or focused breathing, you learn to observe your thoughts, emotions, and bodily sensations without getting caught up in them or reacting impulsively. By cultivating this state of non-judgmental awareness, you can create space between yourself and your traumatic experiences, allowing for a more objective and compassionate perspective.

- *Observing Thoughts and Feelings:* Mindfulness encourages you to observe your thoughts and feelings related to the trauma without judgment or attachment. Instead of getting swept away by distressing thoughts or overwhelming emotions, you practice acknowledging them as passing mental events or sensations. This process can help you develop a greater sense of control over your responses to the trauma and prevent you from becoming overwhelmed by distressing thoughts or emotions.

- *Developing Compassion:* Mindfulness also fosters self-compassion and self-care. By observing your thoughts and feelings without judgment, you can develop a kind and compassionate attitude toward yourself. This includes acknowledging the pain and suffering caused by the trauma, while also recognizing your resilience and strengths. Through self-compassion, you create a nurturing and supportive inner environment that promotes healing and self-acceptance.

- *Relaxation Techniques:* In addition to mindfulness, relaxation techniques play a significant role in trauma recovery. These techniques, such as deep breathing exercises, progressive muscle relaxation, or guided imagery, help induce a state of deep relaxation and reduce the physical and emotional tension associated with trauma. Relaxation practices can soothe the nervous system, promote a sense of safety, and provide a counterbalance to the distressing effects of trauma.

By incorporating mindfulness and relaxation into your daily life, you can gradually build resilience, reduce anxiety and stress, and develop a healthier perspective on your traumatic experiences. Mindfulness practices are often integrated into therapy sessions and can be complemented by additional therapeutic approaches tailored to trauma healing.

5. Eye Movement Therapy

Eye Movement Therapy, specifically referring to Eye Movement Desensitization and Reprocessing (EMDR)[15], is a therapeutic approach used to help individuals process traumatic memories and reduce their negative impact. It involves following the therapist's hand movements, sounds, or other forms of bilateral stimulation (such as tapping or alternating sounds) while focusing on the traumatic experience.

During an EMDR session, the therapist guides you to bring to mind the distressing memory or the traumatic event. As you recall the memory, the therapist will prompt you to track their hand movements or engage with the bilateral stimulation. This back-and-forth eye movement or stimulation is believed to facilitate the brain's natural healing processes.

The eye movements or bilateral stimulation used in EMDR are thought to stimulate both hemispheres of the brain, promoting the integration of fragmented traumatic memories. This process is believed to help the brain reprocess and reorganize the memory, making it less distressing over time.

As you engage in EMDR, you may notice various thoughts, emotions, or physical sensations arising. The therapist encourages you to observe these experiences without judgment and allows them to process naturally. Gradually, the intensity and distress associated with the traumatic memory tend to diminish as the brain makes new connections and associations.

EMDR also incorporates phases of relaxation and grounding exercises to help you feel safe and supported during the process. The therapist may guide you to focus on positive resources or coping strategies to enhance your resilience and well-being.

Chapter Summary

Unresolved traumas can pose substantial obstacles in the journey of creating and seizing second chances. These emotional imprints from distressing events can unconsciously guide our actions and

---

[15] Forrest, M. S., Shapiro, F. (2004). EMDR: The Breakthrough ""Eye Movement"" Therapy For Overcoming Anxiety, Stress, And Trauma. Birleşik Krallık: Basic Books.

decisions, reducing our willingness to embrace new possibilities. Unresolved traumas can also reemerge unexpectedly, creating emotional turmoil and hindering our ability to engage with new opportunities. However, there are various therapeutic strategies that can assist in confronting and processing these traumas, such as talking therapy, eye movement therapy, exposure therapy, cognitive restructuring, and mindfulness and relaxation techniques.

Chapter Lessons

1. Acknowledge the Influence of Traumas: Recognize that unresolved traumas can subtly influence your behaviors and decisions, steering you away from new experiences and second chances.
2. Confront and Process Traumas: Confronting and processing your traumas, though intimidating, is critical for embracing new possibilities. This involves acknowledging the pain, working through the emotional impact, and releasing the traumatic memories.
3. Engage in Therapies: Therapies like talking therapy, eye movement therapy, exposure therapy, and cognitive restructuring can assist in managing and processing traumas. These therapies provide strategies to manage thoughts and emotions related to the trauma, and develop healthy coping mechanisms.
4. Challenge Negative Thoughts: Identify and challenge negative beliefs and thoughts related to the trauma. Replacing them with more positive and realistic thoughts can change how you feel about the trauma and its effects on your life.
5. Practice Mindfulness and Relaxation: Develop awareness and presence in the moment to create a calmer perspective on traumatic experiences. This approach can help you observe your thoughts and feelings without judgment, fostering compassion towards yourself.
6. Prepare for Potential Re-emergence: Traumas can resurface unexpectedly. Being prepared for this possibility and having strategies in place can help manage these moments and reduce their disruptive impact.

Chapter 5 Letting the Light In: The Value of Acceptance and Reaching Out for Help

Life can be challenging, and at times, it can feel overwhelming. We all face difficult decisions, and making the right choice can feel like a daunting task. In these moments, it can be tempting to isolate ourselves and try to handle everything on our own. However, the truth is that we don't have to face our problems alone. Asking for help can be one of the most powerful tools in our arsenal, and it's essential to learn how to use it.

The first step in accepting and embracing the light is acknowledging that we don't have all the answers. It's okay to admit that we're struggling and that we need help. We need to remember that seeking help is a sign of strength, not weakness. Asking for help takes courage, vulnerability, and humility, but it can be the first step towards positive change.

When we ask for help, we open ourselves up to new perspectives and solutions. Sometimes, all we need is a fresh pair of eyes to help us see a problem from a different angle. Other times, we need someone to listen to us without judgment, to validate our feelings and offer support. Asking for help can also provide us with new resources, tools, and strategies to overcome our challenges.

Asking for help can also help us make better decisions. When we're facing a difficult choice, it's easy to get lost in our thoughts and emotions. Seeking the advice of others can help us gain clarity and perspective, enabling us to make more informed decisions. When we're struggling to make a choice, it's important to remember that we don't have to do it alone. Reaching out to friends, family, or a professional can help us find the support and guidance we need.

Making a change can also be challenging, especially when we're trying to break old habits or patterns. Asking for help can be the key to making lasting change. Whether we're trying to quit smoking, lose weight, or improve our mental health, having a support system can make all the difference. We can seek the help of a therapist, join a support group, or enlist the support of friends and family to help us stay accountable and motivated.

Asking for help can also help us build stronger relationships. When we're vulnerable and ask for help, we're showing others that we trust and value them. Asking for help can also help us build empathy and compassion towards others. When we receive help, we're more likely to pay it forward and help others in return.

However, asking for help can also be challenging. We may worry about being judged or perceived as weak. We may feel ashamed or embarrassed about our struggles. We may fear rejection or that our request will burden others. In these moments, it's important to remember that everyone struggles, and asking for help is a normal and healthy part of life.
It's also essential to seek help from the right sources. While friends and family can be an excellent source of support, sometimes, we need the help of a professional. A therapist or counselor can provide us with the tools and strategies we need to overcome our challenges. They can help us identify patterns, work through traumas, and develop new coping mechanisms.

Ultimately, accepting and embracing the light is about recognizing that we're not alone and that there's no shame in asking for help. It's about learning to trust ourselves and others, building resilience, and finding hope and joy in life. In this chapter, we'll explore the power of asking for help and how it can transform our lives. We'll share stories of people who have overcome adversity by seeking help, and we'll provide practical tips and strategies for asking for help and building a support system. Let's take the first step towards the light together.

In the Process of Creating and Seizing a Second Chance

In the process of creating and seizing a second chance, the act of asking for help plays a significant role. Admitting that we don't possess all the answers and recognizing our struggles is the first step towards embracing new possibilities. Far from being a sign of weakness, seeking help underscores one's strength, embodying the courage, vulnerability, and humility necessary to initiate positive change.

When we extend our hands for help, we open ourselves to fresh perspectives and novel solutions. In some instances, a new outlook is all it takes to comprehend a problem differently. In others, we might simply require a supportive ear to validate our emotions without judgment. The act of reaching out can also expose us to new resources, tactics, and strategies that aid in overcoming challenges.

Further, soliciting assistance can enhance our decision-making abilities. Amidst difficult choices, it's effortless to become entangled in our thoughts and emotions, leading to confusion. However, the insights and advice offered by others can shed light on the situation, bringing much-needed clarity and a broader perspective. Therefore, in times of difficult decision-making, it is essential to remember that we are not alone. Connecting with friends, family, or professionals can provide the critical support and guidance necessary to navigate the crossroads and seize a second chance.

The Weight of Perception: Scot's Struggle to Fulfill Family Expectations

Scot was a high school student with a dream. He had always wanted to become an engineer, just like his older brother and his father. In his family, engineering was the gold standard for academic success. Everyone who was considered smart and ambitious went into engineering, and Scot wanted to be no exception.

The only problem was that Scot had never been good at math. Despite his best efforts, he struggled to grasp the concepts of algebra and trigonometry. His grades in math class were consistently poor, and he spent countless hours studying and practicing, but he never seemed to improve.

Despite his lack of math skills, Scot remained determined to pursue a career in engineering. He had set his sights on a prestigious engineering school and spent hours researching the program and the admissions process. He was confident that he

could overcome his shortcomings and prove himself as a worthy candidate.
However, as he began to apply to engineering schools, Scot faced a harsh reality. His grades and test scores were simply not good enough to be admitted to any of the engineering programs he had applied to. He was rejected from every school he had applied to, and his dreams of becoming an engineer began to crumble.

Scot's father and his father's friends began to suggest alternative career paths for him, ones that did not require advanced math skills. They encouraged him to consider fields like business or law, where his strong communication skills and creative thinking could be put to good use.

But Scot refused to listen. He was determined to prove everyone wrong and show that he had what it takes to be an engineer. He poured even more time and effort into studying math, seeking out tutors and taking extra classes. He was convinced that he could improve his skills enough to be admitted to an engineering program.

Despite his unwavering determination, Scot's efforts were in vain. He was once again rejected from every engineering program he applied to. His dream of becoming an engineer was shattered, and he was left feeling lost and directionless.
In the aftermath of his disappointment, Scot began to reflect on his motivations for pursuing engineering. He realized that his desire to be perceived as smart and successful had clouded his judgment and caused him to pursue a career that was not right for him. He had ignored his own interests and strengths in favor of trying to fit in with his family's expectations.

With this newfound awareness, Scot began to explore other career options that aligned more closely with his passions and skills. He discovered a love for creative writing and journalism and began to pursue opportunities in those fields. And while he still felt the sting of his failure to become an engineer, he knew that he had found a path that was true to himself.

A Story of Love, Ego, and Learning to Compromise

Pamela was the cherished only child of her family, raised with utmost care and attention. She was showered with toys, clothes and anything she desired. A diligent student, Pamela excelled in academics and extra-curricular activities, earning numerous awards and honors. She was a star in her family and school. After graduation, Pamela married a handsome man named Matthew whom she had been dating for some time. Unfortunately, their marriage was not the fairytale Pamela had imagined. Matthew had a traditional outlook, and was unaware of household chores, which led to constant disagreements between them. He believed that it was solely the woman's duty to manage the household, which caused friction in their relationship.

Pamela was accustomed to being a decision-maker, and this mindset spilled over into her married life. She refused to compromise on anything, even when it came to trivial matters such as deciding where to eat out. Her uncompromising attitude led to regular arguments between the couple.

Tina, one of Pamela's close friends, advised her to be more understanding towards Matthew. But Pamela was unyielding and believed that they were equal partners in their marriage. She thought Matthew should be more considerate towards her needs, but this only worsened their relationship.

Meanwhile, Matthew started to receive attention from a co-worker named Diana. They began having lunch together every day, and Matthew found himself comparing Diana to Pamela. Matthew and Diana traveled to Hawaii on a business trip, and this brought them closer together. Matthew realized that he was unhappy in his marriage and decided to end things with Pamela.

Pamela was devastated when Matthew left her for another woman. She couldn't comprehend why he would do that to her and would often tell people that Matthew had left her for a colleague. It was a tough lesson for Pamela that being strong and independent didn't always guarantee a happy marriage.

She learned that being a partner meant being open to compromise and understanding, even when it's not what one wants.

In the end, Pamela understood that her stubbornness had cost her the love of her life. She learned that a successful relationship required working together and being willing to compromise.

Trusting the Experts: Aida's Journey from Doubt to Clarity

As a university student, Aida had the fortune of discovering two exceptional part-time job opportunities while searching for an internship. The first option was to work part-time for a local company and earn a decent wage. This was a great opportunity for a university student looking to obtain an internship that would pay a minimum wage. The second option was an unpaid internship with an international company. Everyone advised her to take the latter, as it seemed like a sensible choice. During a visit by an HR manager to the university, Aida confided in them about her situation. The HR manager recommended that she take the internship with the international company. Working for an international company would provide her with an internship that would be recognized and respected globally. On the other hand, working for a local company wouldn't offer as many benefits in terms of international recognition and reputation, as the name of the local company was unknown. What the HR manager said made perfect sense to her. Despite numerous people advising her to intern with a local company, she chose the international one.

After completing her internship, Aida bumped into the general manager of the London office of the international company in an elevator at a conference where she was working. Upon discovering that she had interned with the company before, he offered her the opportunity to continue her internship in London, if she wished to do so.

Lessons Learned

The story of Scot highlights the importance of getting help and accepting guidance when pursuing a career path. Scot's determination to become an engineer despite his poor math skills led to repeated rejection from engineering schools. He refused to listen to his father's and his father's friends' suggestions to consider alternative career paths, convinced that he could improve his math skills enough to be admitted to an engineering program. However, his efforts were in vain, and he was left feeling lost and directionless. It was only after reflecting on his motivations for pursuing engineering that he realized he had been ignoring his own interests and strengths in favor of trying to fit in with his family's expectations.

Scot's story highlights the importance of seeking guidance and advice from others, especially when pursuing a career path. It's essential to listen to the suggestions of those who have more experience and knowledge, even if it means considering alternative career paths. Accepting guidance can help prevent wasted effort and disappointment, and can help an individual discover a career path that aligns with their passions and skills.

The story of Pamela highlights the importance of seeking help and guidance, and being open to compromise in relationships. Pamela's upbringing and academic success had instilled in her a sense of independence and a desire to always be in control. However, this same mindset caused her to be inflexible and unwilling to compromise in her marriage to Matthew. Despite her friend Tina's advice to be more understanding, Pamela was determined to have things her way, leading to constant arguments with Matthew. When Matthew began receiving attention from a co-worker, Pamela's refusal to compromise ultimately led to the end of their marriage. Pamela was devastated and couldn't understand why Matthew would leave her for another woman. It was a tough lesson for her to learn that being strong and independent didn't necessarily equate to a successful relationship. She realized that being open to compromise and understanding was key to a healthy partnership. Pamela's story serves as a reminder that seeking guidance and being open to compromise can lead to better outcomes in relationships. It is important to recognize when our own mindset or actions are causing harm and to be willing to make changes for the betterment of the relationship.

Aida was fortunate to have access to two great part-time job opportunities while looking for an internship during her university studies. However, she struggled to decide which one to choose. Seeking guidance, she confided in an HR manager who visited her university. The HR manager advised her to take the unpaid internship with the international company, which made sense to Aida. This decision later paid off when she met the general manager of the London office of the same international company, who offered her the chance to continue her internship in London. Aida's experience shows the importance of seeking guidance from trusted sources, as it can help individuals make informed decisions that lead to success. It also highlights the value of being open to new opportunities, even if they may not be the obvious choice at first.

From "Can't" to "Can": Overcoming Roadblocks with the Right Help

No matter how intelligent one may be, everyone needs an objective perspective, especially during times of uncertainty or conflict. It is like having a special lamp in a cloudy or smoky environment that helps one see ahead more clearly. However, some people are too proud to ask for help, and they even reject offered help.

Asking for help is crucial, especially during periods of high uncertainty in our lives. It is an advantage if the person who will help us has no personal interest, is outside of the conflict, and has a neutral approach.

People's help can be categorized into two groups: those who say "you can do it" and those who say "you cannot do it." The former can be divided into two sub-groups: those who only say "you can do it" without providing a model and those who explain the reasons and methods for achieving it. The latter can also be divided into two sub-groups: those who only say "you cannot do it" and those who suggest alternative methods.

Three of these four groups are very valuable:

Those who say "you can do it".

Those who say "you can do it with this method".

Those who say "you cannot do it this way, but you can do it this way".

These three approaches allow us to move forward. The last two, on the other hand, help us reach the result by dealing with our method. Therefore, hearing b and c approaches opens our ears, eyes, and hearts, enlightens our path, and fills our sails with the wind.

Therefore, when we hear approaches b and c, we should open our hearts and ears to enlighten our path and fill our sails with the wind.
Of course, if the sails are down, they won't fill with wind. Here, the sails being down is not a metaphor. For a sailboat to move, the sails must actually be raised.
Confronting ourselves is necessary. When an expert tells us that we are going the wrong way or emphasizes a deficiency we need to complete, we should set aside arrogance, self-admiration, or the strange power of not communicating and being closed, and open our hearts and ears.

Looking at all these examples, it is better to listen to the words and efforts of the people around us who try to enlighten us rather than being stubborn and hitting the wall.

Gideon: The Power of Listening

Gideon[16] is a 1998 American romantic tragic comedy starring Christopher Lambert, Charlton Heston and Carroll O'Connor. The **film** was directed by Claudia Hoover. This movie a blueprint to discover the treasure of listening.
The power of listening is often underestimated, but the story of Gideon, a man with the perception level of a child, shows just how transformative it can be. When Gideon is sent to a nursing home full of elderly residents, he approaches each person without prejudice, listening to their stories and feelings without judgment. Through his calm, open-minded personality, he helps others gather and clarify their thoughts, giving them the

---

[16] Hoover, Claudia, dir. Gideon. MGM, 1998.

opportunity to confront themselves and question their situation. Gideon's love for life and desire to live gives other elderly people, who had escaped from life, the will to hold on to life. Gideon's approach to life, which is beyond rigid logical patterns, allows him to interpret things by feeling them. For example, on the first day he arrives, he predicts that the rain, which is predicted to last for days, will stop pouring down like a bucket, and the rain stops just as he said. Gideon's ability to understand everyone and the language of nature shows how being open-minded and attentive can provide a unique perspective on the world.

Gideon's simple questions in an unplanned and childlike manner at the end of conversations help people find out what they need to do, even though he is not a consultant, expert, or therapist. By simply listening and helping others gather their thoughts, he is able to make a real impact on their lives. Furthermore, Gideon's physical appearance and lack of academic intelligence, such as not knowing how to read or write, is not a barrier to his ability to connect with others. In fact, the changes that Gideon creates in the lives of others show that having a big heart is more important than reading, having academic intelligence, physical strength, or professional skills. In the end, despite being aware of his leukemia from the beginning, Gideon clings tightly to his time and shows these people, who feel like they are very close to the end, that life is not just a memory of the past, but a new beginning every day. His ability to listen without judgment and bring hope and inspiration to others is a testament to the power of a positive attitude and the importance of connecting with others on a deeper level.

In conclusion, the story of Gideon shows the transformative power of listening and the impact that a positive attitude can have on the lives of others. By approaching life with an open mind and heart, Gideon was able to make a real difference in the lives of those around him. This story serves as a reminder that we should all strive to listen without judgment, be open to new perspectives, and approach life with positivity and hope.

The "write" Stuff: Jamal's Journey with Pulitzer Prize-Winning Author

The movie "Finding Forrester"[17] highlights the power of mentoring and being open to learning. The film follows the story of Jamal Wallace, a gifted student in the Bronx who downplays his potential and instead spends most of his time playing basketball with his friends. He sneaks into the apartment of William Forrester, a Pulitzer Prize-winning author who has become a neighborhood legend, and leaves his backpack behind. Forrester edits Jamal's personal writings and drops the backpack onto the street, inviting Jamal inside to read more of his writing.

Forrester agrees to help Jamal with his writing, but on the condition that he does not ask about Forrester's life or tell anyone about him. The two bond over writing, with Forrester giving Jamal his own work to rewrite. While Jamal's writing improves, one of his professors suspects him of plagiarism. Despite this, Jamal excels on the basketball court and befriends his classmate Claire. Forrester attends one of Jamal's games but has an anxiety attack and reveals his trauma to Jamal on the empty field at Yankee Stadium.

The movie shows that Forrester's mentoring and guidance help Jamal grow not only as a writer but also as a person. Through his mentorship, Jamal learns about the power of writing and storytelling and develops a deeper understanding of himself and the world around him. He also learns the importance of keeping promises and standing up for what he believes in, even if it means risking his scholarship.

Furthermore, the film highlights the importance of being open to learning and the value of unconventional education. Jamal's education is not limited to what he learns in school but also from his interactions with Forrester, who teaches him about life and writing. Forrester, despite being a recluse, has a wealth of knowledge and experience that he shares with Jamal.

---

[17] Marshall, Gus, dir. Finding Forrester. Touchstone Pictures, 2000.

The movie also highlights the importance of trust in mentorship. Jamal betrays Forrester's trust by taking their writing without permission, which puts their friendship in jeopardy. Forrester is angry and disappointed with Jamal, but in the end, he realizes that Jamal's friendship was worth more than his trust.

In conclusion, "Finding Forrester" emphasizes the power of mentoring and being open to learning. The film shows that a mentor can have a profound impact on a person's life, and that learning can come from unconventional sources. It also underscores the importance of trust in mentorship and the need for honesty and integrity in relationships. Ultimately, the movie encourages us to seek out mentors who can guide and inspire us and to be open to learning from those around us.

Seeing Beyond the Blinders: Listening with Our Hearts

We all have people in our lives who inspire us and help us see things in a new light. These individuals could be anyone from family members to mentors, and they have a unique way of shedding light on us and illuminating our path. However, we often fail to give them the opportunity to do so. By allowing them to enlighten us, we can learn to dream of a better future with the help of friends.

Sometimes, we become so caught up in our own thoughts and worries that we forget to share them with those closest to us. By opening up and letting others see our hopes and dreams, we give them the chance to provide valuable insights and support. Together, we can work towards creating a better future.

When setting goals and aspirations, it's essential to ensure they are realistic and achievable. By aiming for better but not higher ideals, we set ourselves up for success and avoid disappointment. Rather than trying to be someone we're not, we should strive to be the best version of ourselves. Aiming for better but not higher ideals is about finding a balance between reaching our full potential and being true to ourselves. It's easy to get caught up in the pursuit of material success and societal expectations, but true happiness and fulfillment come from aligning our goals with our values and passions. By focusing on personal growth and self-improvement, we can achieve a sense of purpose and fulfillment that extends beyond our careers and material possessions. This approach encourages us to explore our interests and pursue our dreams without the pressure of conforming to external standards. In doing so, we can create a more meaningful and authentic life that reflects our unique aspirations and desires.

Listening is a skill that is often undervalued, but it can have a significant impact on our personal growth and relationships. When we truly listen to others, we gain a better understanding of their perspective and experiences. This not only helps us become more empathetic and compassionate, but it also allows us to grow and become more precious and valuable as individuals.

Effective problem-solving requires collaboration and communication. By listening to others, asking questions, and offering feedback, we can gain a deeper understanding of the issue at hand and work towards finding a solution together. These practices are essential skills for personal and professional growth.

Allowing people who enlighten us to shed light on us, dreaming a better future with the help of friends, aiming for better but not higher ideals, growing and becoming precious and valuable just by listening, and solving problems just by listening and asking questions and providing feedback are all crucial components of personal and professional growth. By embracing these practices, we can become better versions of ourselves and create more meaningful connections with those around us.

Chapter Summary

Life's challenges can sometimes feel overwhelming, causing us to isolate ourselves. However, acknowledging our struggles and seeking help is a sign of strength and the first step towards positive change. Asking for help opens us to new perspectives, solutions, resources, and better decision-making. It also aids in making lasting changes, builds stronger relationships, and promotes empathy and compassion. While it may be difficult due to fear of judgment or burdening others, it's important to remember that seeking help is a normal part of life. Reaching out to the right sources, like friends, family, and professionals, can provide the necessary tools to overcome challenges. Moreover, listening to others is a significant skill that leads to better understanding, empathy, and effective problem-solving.

Chapter Lessons

1. Acknowledge Struggles: Recognize when you're struggling and admit that you need help. Seeking help is a sign of strength, requiring courage, vulnerability, and humility.
2. Be Open to Perspectives: Asking for help can provide fresh perspectives and solutions to problems. It's a resource for gaining new tools and strategies to tackle challenges.
3. Make Better Decisions: Seek advice when facing difficult decisions. It helps gain clarity and perspective, enabling more informed decision-making.
4. Foster Change: When trying to break old habits or make substantial changes, having a support system can be vital. Therapists, support groups, and friends can provide necessary help.
5. Build Stronger Relationships: By showing vulnerability and asking for help, we demonstrate trust in others, strengthening our relationships and fostering empathy and compassion.
6. Overcome Fears: Although asking for help may be challenging due to fear of judgment or rejection, remember that everyone has struggles and seeking help is a normal part of life.
7. Seek Right Sources: Reach out to appropriate sources for help, which can include friends, family, or professionals, depending on the nature of the problem.
8. Practice Listening: Listening effectively helps to understand others better, promotes empathy, and aids in effective problem-solving. It's an important skill for personal growth.
9. Accept and Embrace the Light: Trust yourself and others and build resilience. It's about finding hope and joy in life and understanding that you're not alone in facing challenges.

Chapter 6 The Gifts in Life: How New People and Living Beings Bring Joy and Growth

Humans have a tendency to keep their lives in a closed system, always seeking to define and establish their workplaces, friends, entertainment, and even problems. The comfort and security of routine make us feel at ease with familiar and safe elements, such as a trusted job, a favorite restaurant, music, and beloved friends and family. However, a new person, living being, or thing that enters our system can disrupt the balance, and we may perceive it as a threat. We may readily adapt to a new pet, but we may not be as accepting when our neighbor brings a dog into their apartment.

Fear of the unknown and uncertainty drives us to cling to the familiar and established elements of our personal life system. Yet, we need to realize that a new element entering our system may provide growth opportunities and development. Society's labeling of situations, such as a sick or elderly person who requires our care, may cause us to view them as burdensome. However, this perception impedes us from seeing the value that these individuals can bring to our lives.

Our present-focused viewpoint can also limit us from recognizing the potential of a new element that initially appears to be a burden. For instance, a child who views studying as a burden may not realize the future benefits that it offers. Parenting comes with many difficulties, including sleepless nights and years of service to their children. Yet, most parents do not complain about this service and raise their children with great love and care. Unfortunately, an elderly person who requires similar care may not receive the same level of attention. However, if we view these individuals as gifts, as we do with babies, we could turn from unhappy people to happy people all of a sudden.

To accept new people, living beings, or elements into our lives, we must acknowledge them as gifts. Embracing them, adapting to them, and creating a new life system in which they are included can bring growth, development, and joy. Similarly, adopting a new pet may bring challenges and adjustments, but it can also be a gift that brings joy and companionship into our lives. A pet can provide us with unconditional love, teach us responsibility and empathy, and improve our mental and physical health. The same applies to new people entering our lives, whether it be through work, social activities, or chance encounters. They can bring new ideas, perspectives, and experiences that enrich our lives and help us grow as individuals.

A Newcomer and Creating and Seizing a Second Chance

A newcomer's entrance into our lives, be it a friend, a colleague, a pet, a neighbor, or a relative, can significantly impact our ability to create and seize a second chance. Their introduction offers fresh perspectives, novel interactions, and an alteration in our routine that can be instrumental in generating opportunities for change and growth.

Firstly, a newcomer brings a fresh perspective into our lives. Their views, experiences, and knowledge can challenge our preconceived notions, enabling us to see things from a different angle. This broadening of our worldview can provoke introspection, stimulate new ideas, and inspire us to reconsider our choices, thereby paving the way for a second chance. Secondly, the interaction with a newcomer can disrupt our habitual patterns. Humans are creatures of habit, and often our routines, thought patterns, and behaviors can hinder our ability to recognize and seize opportunities for change. A newcomer, by injecting novelty into our daily lives, can disrupt these routines and provide the impetus for change.

Thirdly, newcomers can provide emotional support and motivation. For instance, a new friend or relative can offer encouragement, empathy, and reassurance during challenging times. A new pet can provide unconditional love and companionship, leading to a boost in morale and emotional well-being. Such emotional upliftment can enhance our resilience and empower us to seize second chances when they present themselves.

Fourthly, newcomers can become allies in our pursuit of a second chance. A new colleague can become a collaborator on a project or provide the necessary assistance to help us advance in our career. A new neighbor may introduce us to a supportive community or local resources that we were previously unaware of, which can open up new opportunities.

In conclusion, the arrival of a newcomer in our lives can instigate a ripple effect of change, triggering introspection, altering routines, enhancing emotional well-being, and providing much-needed support. All these factors collectively create fertile ground for the inception and capture of a second chance.

Let go of your fears!

To truly embrace new gifts in our lives, we need to let go of our fear and resistance to change. We need to approach these new elements with an open mind and heart, willing to adapt and learn from them. We can start by stepping out of our comfort zones and trying new things, meeting new people, and exploring different perspectives. We can also cultivate a sense of gratitude for the gifts we already have in our lives, such as our family, friends, and pets.

In conclusion, taking people and living beings into our lives as gifts can bring immense joy, growth, and fulfillment. By embracing change and approaching new additions to our lives with an open mind, we can create a life system that is vibrant, diverse, and full of opportunities. We can learn from the wisdom of the elderly, the companionship of pets, and the experiences of new people. It is up to us to shift our perspective and see the gifts that exist beyond our routines and comfort zones. Let us welcome each new addition to our lives as a precious gift, one that enriches us and helps us become the best versions of ourselves.

The Unexpected Gift

Raul had always been a man of routine. He liked things to be just so, and he was perfectly content with his solitary life. He had a small shop in the heart of the city, and he was famous for his punctuality and tidiness. His friends often joked that he was the most organized man in the world. But the truth was that Raul just couldn't tolerate other people. He had never gotten married, even though he had been in love once. He just couldn't bear the thought of sharing his life with someone else.

Heart-wrenching sorrow befell Raul's life when tragedy struck one fateful day. A catastrophic car accident claimed the lives of his beloved sister and her entire family, leaving him utterly devastated. He had lost the only family he had left. But then he received a call from the hospital. His nephew, Oliver, a little boy, had been in the car with them, but he had survived. Raul was the only family Oliver had left, and he needed to take care of him.

At first, Raul was hesitant. He had never taken care of a child before, and he had no idea how to do it. But he couldn't turn his back on his nephew. So, he took Oliver in and began to care for him.

At first, it was chaos. Raul's carefully organized life was turned upside down by the little boy's presence. His shop was a mess, and he was constantly running late. But as time went on, Raul began to realize the beauty of having a child in his life. Oliver brought a joy and wonder to his life that he had never known before.

Of course, there were problems. Raul struggled with getting Oliver to eat his vegetables and go to bed on time. He had to juggle taking care of the shop and taking care of the boy. As Raul struggled to adjust to life with a child, he found himself dealing with all kinds of new challenges. Oliver's toys and clothes seemed to be everywhere, and Raul couldn't help but feel like his neat and organized world was falling apart. But despite the chaos, he couldn't help but smile at the adorable little boy who had become such an important part of his life.

One morning, Raul took Oliver to the park and found himself chasing the little boy all around the playground. As he tried to catch him, Raul realized that he was having more fun than he had in years. Oliver's laughter and energy were infectious, and

Raul couldn't help but feel grateful for the chance to experience life through the eyes of a child.

As Raul settled into his new role as a father figure, he found that his love for Oliver grew stronger with each passing day. He enjoyed reading bedtime stories and cuddling with the little boy, and he found himself looking forward to every new adventure that they would embark on together.
In the end, Raul realized that his neat and organized life had been missing something all along: the love and joy that comes with having a family. Thanks to Oliver, Raul had discovered a new kind of happiness, one that he never could have imagined before.

Both Grown in a Garden

Tammy was an elementary school teacher in the heart of New York City. Her life was predictable, and she preferred it that way. She woke up early every day, taught her students, and went home to her tiny apartment. Tammy liked to keep everything in control by keeping everything simple. She had a few close friends, but other than that, she didn't have much of a social life.

That all changed when she met Trevor. He was a brilliant engineer who had just moved to the city for work. They met at a coffee shop, and Tammy was immediately drawn to his easy smile and charming personality. They started dating, and in the beginning, everything was like it was straight out of a romantic movie. They went on long walks in Central Park, held hands while watching the sunset, and spent hours talking on the phone.

On her birthday, Trevor gave Tammy an extraordinary gift. He rented her a hobby garden on the outskirts of the city. Tammy was thrilled with the idea of growing her own vegetables like cucumbers and tomatoes. She had always loved plants, but living in the city meant that she had never had the chance to really take care of them. Trevor's gift opened up a whole new world for her.

But then Covid hit, and everything changed. Trevor was stuck in Australia on a business trip, and Tammy was left alone in the city. She was anxious and scared, but she found solace in her hobby garden. She spent hours tending to her plants, watering them, and watching them grow. It became the biggest joy of her life, a good reason to go out, take care of plants, stay far from people, show passion and love to plants.

As Tammy spent more and more time in her garden, she began to realize that there was more to life than just her job and her routine. She found herself smiling more often, and she felt a newfound sense of purpose. For the first time in a long time, she felt truly alive.

When Trevor finally returned to the city, Tammy was a changed woman. She was no longer content with just keeping everything simple. She wanted to explore new things, take risks, and live her life to the fullest. Trevor was thrilled to see the transformation in her, and they continued to explore the city and try new things together.

In the end, Tammy realized that Trevor's gift had given her more than just a hobby garden. It had given her the courage to step out of her comfort zone and embrace all the beauty and excitement that life had to offer. She would be forever grateful to Trevor for showing her the beauty of living life to the fullest.

"Because of Winn-Dixie"

In the heartwarming film "Because of Winn-Dixie,[18]" directed by Wayne Wang, the narrative beautifully unfolds around the theory that every living being that enters our lives can be a gift, waiting to be unpacked and cherished.

The story revolves around 10-year-old India Opal Buloni, who has recently moved to a small town in Florida with her father, known as The Preacher. Opal's mother, who abandoned them

---

[18] Wang, Wayne, dir. Because of Winn-Dixie. 20th Century Fox, Walden Media, 2005.

when she was just three, casts a shadow of sadness over her father, as he remains deeply in love with her despite her absence. Opal sees her father as a turtle, retreating into his own shell and unwilling to engage with the world.

One day, while at the supermarket, Opal encounters a scruffy dog wreaking havoc. Seeing something special in the dog's eyes, Opal decides to take him home and names him Winn-Dixie, after the supermarket where they met. This simple act of compassion and connection marks the beginning of a transformative journey for Opal and those around her.

Opal discovers that every being she encounters has a story to share, just like Miss Franny Block, the librarian, who regales Opal with tales of her great-grandfather. He invented candies that combined sweetness with a tinge of sadness, reflecting the human experience. Opal also learns about the tragic loss of Amanda Wilkinson's younger brother and vows to be kinder to her, realizing the importance of empathy and understanding.

Through her newfound friendship with Winn-Dixie, Opal grows in resilience and compassion. She takes on odd jobs to earn money for a dog collar, works at the pet store with the initially reluctant Otis, who has a troubled past but possesses a kind heart. Otis shares his love for music, soothing the animals with his guitar and revealing the power of healing through art.

Opal's encounters continue as she meets Gloria Dump, a wise and recovering alcoholic. Opal and Gloria forge a deep bond and decide to host a party, mirroring the one in "Gone with the Wind." The event becomes an opportunity for reconciliation, as Opal extends invitations to former adversaries, the Dewberry brothers, as well as Amanda Wilkinson and Sweetie Pie Thomas. The party serves as a catalyst for connection and acceptance, bringing people and their shared experiences together.

Amidst the festivities, Opal realizes that Winn-Dixie is missing, prompting a frantic search. The joyous reunion occurs when she discovers that he had sought shelter from the storm, hidden in

Gloria's home all along. The story concludes with Otis strumming his guitar, filling the room with music as everyone joins in singing one of The Preacher's songs.

"Because of Winn-Dixie" beautifully captures the essence of the theory that every living being can be a gift waiting to be unpacked. Through Opal's journey of compassion, understanding, and friendship, the film reminds us of the transformative power of connection and the importance of embracing the diverse experiences and stories that each individual brings into our lives.

Discovering the Gifts Within Life's Unexpected Additions

In our journey through life, it is natural for us humans to seek comfort and security in our familiar routines and established systems. We tend to define and control every aspect of our lives, from our workplaces and friendships to our sources of entertainment and even our problems. We are often reluctant to let anything, or anyone disrupt this equilibrium, fearing the unknown and uncertainty that comes with change.

However, it is essential for us to recognize that every new person, living being, or element that enters our lives has the potential to bring growth, development, and joy. While we may readily adapt to a new pet, we might be less accepting when our neighbor introduces a dog into their apartment. Our fear of the unknown can lead us to cling tightly to our established elements, preventing us from realizing the value that these new additions can offer.

We tend to label situations and people, often seeing those who require our care or attention, such as the sick or elderly, as burdensome. Society's perceptions influence our perspective, hindering us from appreciating the unique gifts and insights they can bring to our lives. Similarly, our present-focused viewpoint may blind us to the potential benefits that initially burdensome elements, like studying for a child, can provide in the future.

It is crucial for us to shift our mindset and view every person, living being, or element that enters our lives as a precious gift. By embracing and adapting to these new additions, we can create a more vibrant and diverse life system that offers growth, development, and joy. Just as adopting a new pet may present challenges and adjustments, it can also bring immense joy, companionship, and valuable life lessons. The same applies to new people entering our lives, whether through work, social activities, or chance encounters. Each individual has the potential to bring new ideas, perspectives, and experiences that enrich our lives and help us grow as individuals.

To truly embrace these gifts, we must let go of our fears and resistance to change. It requires approaching new elements with an open mind and heart, willing to adapt and learn from them. Stepping out of our comfort zones, trying new things, meeting new people, and exploring different perspectives are all ways to cultivate gratitude and appreciation for the gifts we already have in our lives.

By acknowledging and accepting new people, living beings, or elements as gifts, we open ourselves up to immense joy, growth, and fulfillment. Let us shift our perspective, welcoming each new addition as a precious gift that enriches our lives and helps us become the best versions of ourselves. It is through this openness and willingness to embrace change that we can create a life system full of opportunities, diversity, and meaningful connections.

Chapter Summary

People tend to seek security and comfort in the familiar elements of their lives, which can lead to resistance when something new disrupts this balance. Fear of the unknown can cause us to view these changes as threats rather than opportunities for growth and development. It is important to shift our perspectives and consider every new element as a gift that can bring enrichment and joy to our lives. Embracing and adapting to these changes can lead to a more vibrant and diverse life, filled with new ideas, perspectives, and experiences. This requires us to let go of fears and resistances, approach changes with an open mind and heart, and step out of our comfort zones.

Chapter Lessons

1. Embrace the Unfamiliar: We should learn to accept new elements in our lives, understanding that they can provide opportunities for growth and development.
2. Redefine Burdens: Situations or individuals labeled as burdens by society could bring value to our lives if we shift our perception.
3. Appreciate Potential: Avoid a present-focused viewpoint that fails to recognize the future benefits of new elements.
4. Shift Perceptions: Treat every new person or element in your life as a gift, rather than a threat, to experience sudden happiness.
5. Adapt: Adjust your life system to include new elements, embracing the growth, development, and joy they bring.
6. Recognize Value: New people, pets, or situations can bring joy, companionship, and valuable life lessons, teaching us responsibility and empathy and improving our mental and physical health.
7. Let Go of Fears: Overcome your resistance to change and approach new elements with an open mind and heart, willing to adapt and learn from them.
8. Step Out of Comfort Zones: Embrace new experiences, meet new people, and explore different perspectives to cultivate gratitude and appreciation for the gifts in your life.

Chapter 7 Believing in Miracles

If a person truly desires to achieve something and believes in it wholeheartedly, the brain's nerve cells program the entire body to work towards the realization of that goal, thereby altering the boundaries of what is deemed possible. As individuals progress towards their self-determined objectives, they can transform obstacles into opportunities, activate dormant potentials in their surroundings, and push their bodies to surpass their usual capabilities.

Rather than following an uncertain path from causes to outcomes, akin to spreading the available time across a task, a more effective approach involves starting from the desired result and tracing the process of how the underlying reasons come together. If the outcome is inevitable and not merely a possibility or uncertainty, and if individuals genuinely believe that it is not an open-ended endeavor, they must wholeheartedly commit to fulfilling the necessary requirements.

Let's consider the case of a student who neglects their school lessons, lacks enthusiasm for studying, and struggles to maintain focus. In this scenario, imagine that a few days before an exam, they manage to acquire photocopies of class notes for a subject they have never attended. Due to their lack of classroom participation, they don't have any friends who can provide assistance. However, these obtained notes prove challenging to decipher, given their unfamiliarity with the subject matter and the poor quality of the photocopies. The student already faces concentration issues and harbors a negative perception of studying. The subject in question is "Quantative Methods," filled with complex concepts unfamiliar to them. Consequently, upon a cursory glance at the initial pages, they feel overwhelmed, their confidence plummets, and they convince themselves that they are incapable of succeeding. As a result, they decide not to study, skip the exam, or submit a blank paper.

Later on, there is a final exam for the same course. Failure to pass this exam would result in prolonged schooling, doubled tuition fees, rejection of financial support from his out-of-town family, or the inability to fulfill his summer plans to study abroad, which necessitates maintaining a specific grade average. However, if a genuine belief and unwavering certainty take root in his mind regarding the accomplishment he seeks, studying and comprehending the course material become attainable objectives.

Despite his initial scattered thoughts and struggles with focus, "Quantitative Methods" becomes the most prominent preoccupation in his mind. Seeking assistance from others, which previously seemed burdensome, now becomes an accessible option aligned with his aspirations. He might invest in supportive and enlightening study materials, and as he immerses himself in the seemingly complex topics, he begins to discover interconnections among them, though not comprehending the entirety of the subject matter but perceiving solvable enigmas within specific aspects. He secures access to previous exam questions, an invaluable resource for his preparation. As the subject matter that previously appeared daunting now holds the status of an anticipated achievement, a clear direction emerges for his efforts, and he gradually realizes that the perceived difficulty dissipates once he unravels the underlying principles.

The disparity in effort between achieving an excellent grade and simply passing a course is minimal. Only a select few manage to pass with an outstanding grade, while nearly the entire student body finds a way to pass the course, even if it takes them a second or third attempt. If obtaining a very high grade were a prerequisite for passing the course, the number of individuals achieving such a grade would be significantly higher. In theory, everyone aspires to attain a high grade, but only a handful truly believe in it and work diligently, considering it a necessity and having confidence in their ability to succeed. The majority of us settle for meeting the minimum requirements because that is the extent of our belief. Just as everyone has a place to live, only a few possess a considerable amount of wealth that could be deemed substantial.

When a newborn baby is immersed in water, they instinctively float and remain on the surface, whereas an adult who lacks swimming skills panics, struggles, and sinks further, convinced they might drown. Their inability to coordinate their body and exhibit the appropriate response stems from conditioned behavior. Regrettably, this inclination to panic and succumb to despair persists even in situations that could naturally resolve themselves.

The Story of Zahra and the Law of Attraction

Merely wishing for something in life without taking any action seems unlikely to help individuals achieve their desires, unless serendipitous events occur.

Let's consider Zahra as an example. Zahra has a deep aspiration to become a "film director." She immerses herself in the world of cinema, watching movies, reading books about filmmaking, and avidly following interviews with acclaimed directors. At night, she envisions herself as a successful filmmaker. Zahra's passion to become a film director is unwavering. However, she finds herself working as an accountant in a company and, over the years, retires from her accounting career without fulfilling her dream.

Now, let's explore a fortuitous scenario for Zahra. By chance, Zahra decides to leave her accounting job and serendipitously secures a position as an accountant in a film production company. It is during this time that her boss discovers one of her scripts on his desk and inquires about its author. Zahra enthusiastically shares her vision for the film, and to her surprise, her boss perceives her talent and offers her the opportunity to bring her vision to life as a director. Zahra successfully transitions from accounting to directing.

Now, let's delve into a version where Zahra truly focuses on her goal. In this iteration, Zahra goes beyond merely watching films, reading books, and studying interviews. She vocalizes her ambition to become a director, attends filmmaking courses, writes and submits scripts to production companies, seeks out connections with industry professionals, enhances her language skills to communicate effectively, and actively engages with the film community. Through her perseverance, Zahra earns a position as an assistant director, propelling her further into the realm of cinema.

It is in this third version, where Zahra demonstrates focused determination, that the "Law of Attraction" comes into play. However, if one solely daydreams and relies on desire without taking concrete steps towards their goals, success becomes a matter of chance. It is essential to recognize that organized effort and action are vital components of achieving one's aspirations.

The book, The Law of Attraction, as depicted in the above, presents a simplified and unrealistic portrayal of achieving goals. While the book may resonate with individuals who believe that simply desiring something will make it manifest in their lives, it fails to address the crucial aspect of taking proactive and organized action.

The example of Zahra's journey illustrates the limitations of relying solely on the Law of Attraction. In the first scenario, Zahra's unwavering desire to become a film director does not translate into success because she does not actively pursue her goal. This challenges the notion that sheer wishing and visualization alone can lead to the realization of one's aspirations.

Furthermore, the book overlooks the importance of perseverance, skill development, and strategic planning. Zahra's eventual success in the second and third scenarios is not a result of chance or the Law of Attraction magically aligning the universe in her favor. Instead, her achievements stem from her decision to actively seek opportunities, enhance her knowledge and skills, build connections, and persistently pursue her passion. These elements of effort and dedication are fundamental to achieving success, which the Law of Attraction fails to acknowledge.

Critics argue that the Law of Attraction can promote a passive mindset, fostering the belief that one can simply wish for their desires to materialize without putting in the necessary work. It neglects the reality that accomplishing goals often requires determination, resilience, and deliberate action.

Moreover, the book's omission of the importance of realistic goal-setting and adaptability can mislead readers. Zahra's story highlights the significance of adapting her career path from accounting to film production, demonstrating the need to adjust strategies when faced with unforeseen circumstances. The Law of Attraction's focus on positive thinking and visualization alone disregards the complexities of real-life challenges and the need for a well-rounded approach to achieving goals.

In conclusion, the Law of Attraction, as portrayed in the above text, oversimplifies the process of achieving goals by emphasizing wishful thinking and visualization while neglecting the crucial role of active effort, skill development, perseverance, and adaptability. It is important for individuals seeking success to recognize the limitations of relying solely on the Law of Attraction and instead embrace a more comprehensive and grounded approach to pursuing their aspirations.

The Maldonado Miracle

The Maldonado Miracle is a film that explores the power of helping, and creating miracles through belief, effort, and connection rather than relying on divine intervention. The story revolves around Jose, a Mexican boy searching for his father who is working as an undocumented laborer. Jose's journey leads him to the struggling town of San Ramos, where he hides in a church attic and unintentionally causes a phenomenon of blood tears on the statue of Jesus.

The film highlights the transformative effects of the supposed miracle on both the individuals in the town and the visitors who come seeking miracles of their own. It portrays how acts of kindness, hope, and belief can inspire people to go beyond their ordinary lives and make extraordinary efforts to connect with others and create positive change. The characters in the film, such as Stella, Lyle, Maise, and Cruz, each have their own personal struggles and desires, and the miracle serves as a catalyst for their journeys of self-discovery, connection, and growth.

One of the film's key messages is the power of human agency and the potential for miracles to be created through human effort and connection. The film challenges the notion that miracles can only be attributed to divine intervention and instead suggests that the power of hope, helping, and believing in oneself and others can be equally transformative. It emphasizes the importance of taking the extra step, going beyond one's comfort zone, and showing kindness and compassion to others, as these actions can have a profound impact on individuals and communities.

The Maldonado Miracle also touches upon the themes of faith, belief, and the power of perception. While some characters, like the priest, struggle to understand the origin of the miracle and seek logical explanations, others wholeheartedly embrace the belief in miracles, finding solace, purpose, and renewed faith in the presence of the supernatural. The film challenges traditional notions of faith and miracles, suggesting that they can exist in the realm of human experience and effort rather than relying solely on divine intervention.

Unstoppable Bonds

In a small town nestled among rolling hills, there lived a loving family: Sarah, John, and their daughter Emily. They led a happy and contented life until tragedy struck on a stormy night. The family was driving home from a vacation when their car skidded off the road, crashing into a tree. Sarah and John miraculously survived, but Emily, their precious daughter, fell into a deep coma.

Days turned into weeks, and weeks into months, but Emily showed no signs of waking up. The doctors did their best, but their prognosis grew bleaker with each passing day. Sarah and John refused to accept their daughter's fate and began a desperate search for a miraculous cure. They scoured medical journals, sought out alternative therapies, and consulted specialists from around the world. Yet, no treatment seemed to offer any hope.

While browsing the internet in search of a breakthrough, Sarah stumbled upon a story about a renowned healer named Dr. Elena. According to the accounts, Dr. Elena possessed the gift of healing, having helped countless individuals recover from seemingly incurable conditions. Filled with renewed hope, Sarah convinced John to embark on a journey to find Dr. Elena.

Their quest led them to a remote village nestled deep in the mountains. The village was shrouded in mystery, and its inhabitants spoke of Dr. Elena's miraculous abilities with reverence. Sarah and John were determined to reach her, no matter the obstacles that lay in their path.

The journey was treacherous, with rugged terrain and harsh weather conditions testing their resolve. But the couple persevered, driven by their unwavering love for their daughter. Along the way, they encountered kind-hearted strangers who offered assistance, providing them with shelter, food, and directions.

Finally, after days of relentless travel, Sarah and John arrived at Dr. Elena's humble abode. The healer greeted them with compassion and listened intently to their tale of woe. She explained that Emily's condition was indeed grave but reassured them that miracles were possible if they believed with all their hearts.

She was known for her unconventional and distinctive methods that had helped countless people overcome seemingly insurmountable odds. Dr. Elena believed in the power of combining ancient wisdom with modern medicine, harnessing the body's innate healing abilities. Determined to help the Anderson family, she offered her expertise.

Dr. Elena arrived at the hospital with an air of tranquility surrounding her. She began by infusing the room with the soothing scent of lavender and chamomile, using aromatherapy to create a peaceful environment. Sarah and John breathed in the calming fragrance, feeling a glimmer of hope wash over them.

Next, Dr. Elena introduced sound therapy into Emily's treatment. She played ethereal melodies that resonated with healing frequencies, filling the room with gentle harmonies. The vibrations seemed to dance through Emily's body, as if whispering messages of restoration and renewal.

Knowing the power of nature, Dr. Elena prepared a custom blend of herbal remedies tailored to Emily's needs. She carefully selected herbs known for their rejuvenating.

But Dr. Elena's methods went beyond the physical. She understood the importance of addressing the emotional and energetic aspects of healing. With gentle touch and focused intention, she performed energy healing, allowing her healing energy to flow through her hands and into Emily's body. Sarah and John could feel a warm current of energy passing through them as they witnessed the transformative power of Dr. Elena's touch.

As the days turned into weeks, Dr. Elena guided Sarah, John, and Emily in visualization exercises and positive affirmations. Together, they envisioned Emily's body vibrant and healthy, filled with radiant light. They repeated affirmations of healing and strength, nurturing their belief that Emily's recovery was within reach.

Days turned into weeks, and slowly but surely, Emily began to stir from her slumber. Her eyes fluttered open, revealing a glimmer of recognition. Sarah and John couldn't contain their joy as they witnessed their daughter's miraculous awakening.

The Formula of Miracles

I have been studying individuals who have experienced remarkable outcomes in their lives that can be considered as miracles. Who are the ones that these miracles happen to?

First and foremost, miracles occur to those who firmly believe in their possibility. Those who hold the belief that the impossible can become possible are proven right, while those who doubt it continue on their path of ordinary existence. Conversely, those who wholeheartedly embrace the notion that the impossible can be achieved, and actively strive for it, witness the realization of these extraordinary feats and embark on a life that defies convention.

During my seminars, I conduct an experiment centered around the concept of impossibility. I present a physical challenge to the participants, involving a straw and an exceedingly soft thin thread. I ask the participants to take the thread through the straw. Initially, the participants perceive the given task as unattainable simply by looking at the pipette and the thread. The experiment is limited to a brief 15-second timeframe. One by one, the participants endeavor to solve the problem using the straw and the thread, but despite their efforts, they are unable to succeed within the given time frame. Even if they were to persist for a few minutes, the task appears insurmountable.

At the midpoint of the experiment, I reveal that I have successfully solved the problem in five distinct ways within a mere one or two seconds. Although the participants learn that the problem can indeed be solved, they still lack faith in their own ability to do so. However, towards the end of the experiment, a single individual accomplishes the task in just one second. Subsequently, I inquire about the initial thoughts of each participant: "Did you believe you could do it? Or did you believe you couldn't?" Those who were unable to succeed express their belief that the problem was inherently impossible from the moment they held the straw and the thread, whereas those who triumphed affirm their unwavering belief in their own capability from the very beginning. This phenomenon exemplifies that those who doubt the possibility of encountering miracles in their lives do not experience them, while those who possess a steadfast belief contribute to the manifestation of such miracles.

Furthermore, let me offer a definition of miracles through the lens of engineering logic. A miracle can be likened to a scenario where we have a specific goal, requiring 100 units to achieve it, while we possess a mere two units. Completing the remaining 98 units seems overwhelmingly improbable. However, if these missing 98 units can somehow be accomplished, a situation akin to a miracle arises. Allow me to provide some examples of outcomes that can be considered as miraculous: an average student gaining admission to Harvard University's esteemed graduate program, an individual who suffered a paralyzing motorcycle accident and was told they would forever rely on crutches defying the odds and recovering to become a role model for exceptional dancers and athletes, the triumphant defeat of a hundred-thousand-strong army by a battalion of three hundred, the hand delivery of a document to a location two hundred kilometers away within a mere hour, and so forth.

The characteristics of those who encounter such extraordinary outcomes in their lives can be summarized as follows:

First and foremost, they have defined for themselves what constitutes a miracle. When I pose the question of what a miracle would entail in their lives, I often receive no immediate response. Therefore, before we can ascertain what can be deemed a miracle, we must first provide an answer to the question, "If there were to be a miracle in your life, what would it look like?"

Secondly, they wholeheartedly believe that the miracle will transpire. As previously mentioned, those who lack belief do not witness miracles.

Thirdly, regardless of how seemingly futile it may appear, they put forth considerable effort. Even when faced with a scenario where we possess a mere three hundred soldiers against an army of one hundred thousand, the most sensible course of action is to pursue the most intelligent strategy available. It is essential to persist without wavering, even if others ridicule us or every endeavor is met with rejection. The animated film "Mulan" highlights how a determined young Chinese girl defeats a colossal Mongol army. Likewise, Genghis Khan overcame the seemingly impassable Great Wall of China and conquered Beijing.

Fourthly, to achieve a miracle, one must work harder than anyone else. Merely exerting the same amount of effort as others does not result in a miracle.

Lastly, and perhaps most crucially, is the power of helping. If our own miracles are to materialize through the aid, support, and understanding of others, then we must reciprocate by assisting in the emergence of miracles and positive outcomes in the lives of others.

Chapter Summary
The power of belief and desire in achieving one's goals are crucial in creating miracles. When a person wholeheartedly believes in and desires something, the brain programs the body to work towards that goal, potentially pushing past previously perceived limits.

A more effective approach to achieving goals is to start with the end result in mind, and then trace the process back to the present. This mindset, along with a firm belief in the inevitability of the desired outcome, can lead to significant success. the difference in effort between merely crossing the finish line and claiming a spot among the top three finishers is marginal. It is the intensity of belief and commitment that distinguishes the high achievers from the rest, acting as the vital catalyst for extraordinary accomplishment.

Chapter Lessons

1. Power of Belief: Wholehearted belief in a goal programs the brain and body to work towards its realization, pushing beyond established boundaries.

2. Transforming Obstacles into Opportunities: Challenges should be viewed as catalysts for unlocking dormant potential and exceeding usual capabilities.

3. Starting with the End in Mind: Effective goal accomplishment involves visualizing the desired outcome and working backwards, tracing the process of how the reasons come together.

4. Importance of Genuine Commitment: When the desired outcome is viewed as inevitable and not just a possibility, one can fully commit to fulfilling the requirements.

5. Impact of Necessity on Achievement: The urgency and necessity of achieving a goal can facilitate focused efforts and eventual success, as illustrated in the case of the hypothetical student.

6. Potential of Miracles: Miracles can occur when individuals define what they consider a miracle, truly believe in its occurrence, put forth significant effort, work harder than others, and actively help others.

7. Role of Effort in Success: There is minimal disparity in effort between achieving excellence and merely passing, suggesting that everyone has the potential for high achievement if they truly commit to it.

8. Fear as a Barrier: Fear can inhibit natural problem-solving responses and lead to panic and despair, as demonstrated in the comparison of a newborn's instinctive float response and an adult's fear-driven sinking response.

9. Importance of Reciprocity: If one expects help, support, and understanding from others in the realization of their miracles, they should also help others in achieving their positive outcomes.

Chapter 8 Learning Through Journeys

When individuals seek to make a change in their lives but find themselves lacking the inner strength to do so, they often turn to psychologists or personal development courses. However, only a few recognize the profound potential for personal transformation that lies within embarking on a journey.

The concept of a journey has evolved with the progress of technology. In the past, a journey from one city to another would take two to three days by horse-drawn carriage, but now intercontinental travel can be completed in less than 24 hours. For instance, a pilgrimage from Turkey can now be accomplished in a mere 14 days, including transportation. In the era of the Ottoman Empire, these journeys could last for months, preventing even the caliphs, who held the highest authority, from embarking on a pilgrimage.

The allure of longer journeys, which used to grant ample opportunities for encountering new people and reflecting on the events along the way, has dwindled in modern times. Today, we can board a plane in Istanbul and arrive in New York within 10 hours, eliminating the chances for an extensive range of experiences during travel.

However, when we speak of journeys, it is crucial to consider those that surpass mundane routine trips. Routine journeys, with their predictable risks and foreseeable developments, can be managed as one is well-prepared for such occurrences. Although routine journeys offer opportunities for personal growth, unexpected events have a lesser impact. Yet, even within the confines of a predictable journey, an unforeseen incident can dramatically alter its course.

The lack of profound learning during our daily commute from work to home, and vice versa, stems from the scarcity of encountering challenges or incidents along the way. On the contrary, embarking on a lengthy voyage to uncharted territories presents numerous opportunities for growth and self-discovery. For example, two young individuals traveling by train in Europe may plan to retrieve their luggage from the storage facility after 8 p.m., only to find out that it closes at 6 p.m. This unforeseen circumstance renders them unable to leave the city without their belongings or spend the night utilizing the contents of their suitcase.

At times, we consult a ferry schedule to determine its departure time, only to arrive at the dock and discover its absence. Unbeknownst to us, we were consulting the weekday schedule while it is, in fact, a Sunday. A seemingly trivial detail can have a profound impact on the entire journey. Moreover, when faced with the challenge of carrying a 70-pounds suitcase up a malfunctioning escalator, a compassionate stranger may come to our aid. Conversely, when we find ourselves perplexed after realizing our wallet has been stolen just as we are about to board a bus, the bus driver strictly enforces the no-ticket-no-entry policy while other passengers turn a blind eye to our plight.

Out of Our Comfort Zone

Journeys, as they say, take us out of our comfort zones. Just as we cannot find the same warmth and ease we experience at home, we cannot expect the same level of comfort during our travels. When our car breaks down on a deserted road during a torrential downpour, we suddenly realize how minuscule we are in this vast universe. Our titles as professors, politicians, or CEOs offer no shield against the elements.

Journeys, figuratively speaking, strip us bare and teach us the most valuable lessons in life. In our vulnerable and impoverished state, we become reliant on love, protection, and assistance. These moments of helplessness allow us to draw closer to both God and our fellow human beings.

Passing through customs, we learn the consequences of filling out a form incorrectly or forgetting to complete a required section. We learn the importance of politely declining food offered by strangers, as it may contain substances that could induce drowsiness. We witness the callousness of customs or visa officials. One of the invaluable lessons learned during journeys is the art of planning. If we feel the absence of something on one journey, we make sure to bring it along on the next. Some of us also learn to let go of unnecessary baggage on future travels.

The most precious gifts of journeys lie in the events that unfold along the way. These events take us out of the monotonous routines of our daily lives. At times, we become mere spectators, while other times, we become victims. We may witness a theft or find ourselves unfortunate victims of stolen belongings or money. Observing how situations are resolved or left unresolved after witnessing someone falling ill or being involved in an accident can be highly instructive.

Another characteristic of journeys is their ability to cultivate patience within us. Waiting for a broken-down bus or train to be repaired, or enduring an endless journey, can test and enhance our patience. Journeys also teach us about our dietary choices. Experiencing diarrhea or an upset stomach during a trip helps us understand what foods we should avoid.

Above all, journeys provide an opportunity for reflection and deep thought, especially when undertaken alone. It can be said that in the fast-paced hustle and bustle of daily life, we rarely allow ourselves the luxury of profound contemplation. However, every journey, devoid of distractions such as television and constant conversations, offers us a chance for introspection. This opportunity can be utilized to review our personal lives, evaluate our mistakes, or plan for the future.

Indeed, a journey can be a marvelous opportunity to ponder and evaluate all these aspects.

Journeys as tools to create and seize a second chance

Journeys play a pivotal role in both creating and seizing a second chance by providing transformative experiences, opportunities for self-reflection, and life lessons that shape our character and decision-making.

A journey, metaphorically or literally, takes us beyond the confines of our daily routines and pushes us to navigate unfamiliar terrains. This sense of uncertainty and novelty that accompanies any journey can serve as a catalyst for change. Whether we are active participants or passive observers, the varied experiences along the journey, such as witnessing a theft or dealing with a delay, can foster adaptability and resilience. These experiences may shift our perspectives, offer us profound insights, and prompt us to reconsider our choices, thereby creating an environment ripe for second chances.

A journey inherently cultivates patience and resilience. Being stranded because of a broken-down vehicle, enduring long waits, or adjusting to unforeseen circumstances are challenging experiences that can test and strengthen our patience. These qualities are crucial when it comes to seizing a second chance, as they help us to stay focused, persistent, and positive in the face of adversity.

In addition to character-building, journeys often lead us to reevaluate our lifestyle choices. For instance, getting sick due to inappropriate food choices during a journey can encourage us to reassess our dietary habits. This shift towards healthier living can pave the way for a second chance towards better physical well-being.

Furthermore, journeys provide an invaluable opportunity for self-reflection and introspection. The moments of solitude and tranquility that journeys often afford can be harnessed to ponder our actions, reassess our goals, and plan our future. Such reflective contemplation can help us identify areas in our lives that require change, thereby revealing potential second chances.

Lastly, journeys tend to inspire a greater appreciation for the diverse facets of life and can help us become more open to change and opportunities. These experiences can broaden our horizons, allowing us to see beyond our current circumstances and embrace the possibility of a second chance.

Non-routine journeys

Non-routine journeys possess several distinct characteristics that contribute to personal transformation. If we are fortunate, these journeys, brimming with challenges and obstacles, draw us closer to others — those we share the journey with and those dear to us. At times, these adversities unite us with our loved ones, unveiling our most humane qualities. The journey exposes both the virtues and flaws that lay concealed beneath the surface of our everyday lives, prompting us to embrace the positive and relinquish the negative.

Furthermore, journeys have the remarkable ability to soften our hardened hearts. Along the way, we shrink in significance, resembling a grain of sand with little influence. The once proud and self-assured individual becomes vulnerable and humble, opening themselves to seek assistance and displaying acts of kindness. Particularly during moments of helplessness, we come to appreciate the significance of experiences that extend beyond the confines of our familiar existence.

Moreover, a prolonged journey, enriched with a series of life-altering encounters, often facilitates the creation of a new and revitalized life for many individuals.

Walking Spirits on the Himalayas

The story of the movie "Himalaya"[19], directed by Eric Valli, demonstrates how journeys can foster personal growth and transformation. Set in the challenging terrain of the Nepalese Himalayas, the narrative follows the villagers who undertake a perilous journey with a yak caravan to trade rock salt for grain. Throughout the film, the characters navigate a series of physical and emotional obstacles, ultimately revealing the profound impact of their journey on their individual and collective growth.

---

[19] Valli, Éric, dir. Himalaya: L'Enfance d'un chef. Pathé Renn Productions, 1999.

The journey begins with a tragic incident: the death of Lhakpa, the heir to the tribe's chieftainship, while attempting a risky shortcut. This event sets the stage for a power struggle and rivalry between the aging chief, Tinle, and the young and audacious herdsman, Karma. As they vie for leadership of the caravan, fueled by misunderstandings and mistrust, their actions and decisions shape the trajectory of their personal growth.

Karma, seeking to prove his worth as a leader, defies the traditional norms and leaves before the scheduled departure, causing unrest among the tribe. Despite objections from Tinle, who believes someone else should lead the caravan, Karma sets out with determination. This act of courage and defiance highlights his desire for growth and self-discovery.

Throughout the arduous journey, Tinle's perseverance and resilience are tested. He faces physical exhaustion and the challenges of keeping the caravan together. In contrast, Karma becomes a role model to Tinle's grandson, Tserin, embodying the spirit of adventure and determination. As the story unfolds, the characters' roles and dynamics evolve, showcasing their individual growth and the transformation of their relationships.

The pivotal moment occurs when a snowstorm threatens the caravan's survival. Tinle, despite his fatigue, leads the group, demonstrating his leadership and the wisdom gained from his experiences. Karma, realizing his earlier mistake, returns to support Tinle and carries him to the front of the caravan. This act of compassion and humility symbolizes Karma's growth and maturity.

As the journey progresses, the characters face the harsh realities of the mountains and the fragility of life. Tinle, recognizing his limitations, requests to be left behind to peacefully pass away in the mountains, aligning with the tribe's belief in honoring the mountains as masters of their destiny.

The story of "Himalaya" underscores how journeys, both physical and metaphorical, provide opportunities for self-discovery, resilience, and personal transformation. Through the challenges they face and the bonds they form, the characters learn valuable lessons about trust, leadership, and the interconnectedness of their lives. Ultimately, the journey through the Himalayas becomes a catalyst for growth, shaping their identities and leaving a lasting impact on their individual and collective consciousness.

Growing on the Tracks

The movie "Tracks"[20], directed by John Curran, showcases how a transformative journey can foster personal growth and self-discovery. Set in the harsh desert of Western Australia, the story follows Robyn Davidson, a young Australian woman, as she embarks on a solitary trek of 2,700 kilometers from Alice Springs to the ocean. Accompanied only by her dog and four camels, Robyn sets out with the intention of challenging herself and finding her true self along the way.

The journey begins with Robyn's determination to venture into the wilderness, leaving behind the comforts of society. She faces initial challenges, such as finding camels and learning to handle them, while encountering skepticism from those around her. Despite the doubts and setbacks, Robyn remains committed to her quest for personal growth and embarks on the journey alone.

Throughout the trek, Robyn's interactions with various individuals shape her perspective and challenge her beliefs. She meets Rick Smolan, an American photographer who becomes fascinated by her journey and offers support. Their evolving relationship provides Robyn with both companionship and moments of frustration, as she grapples with her desire for solitude and independence.

---

[20] Curran, John, dir. Tracks. Roadshow Entertainment, 2013.

As Robyn traverses the unforgiving desert landscape, she faces physical hardships and emotional turmoil. She battles extreme weather conditions, endures personal loss, and confronts her own limitations. These trials push her to the edge of her resilience, testing her resolve and forcing her to confront her fears and insecurities.

Robyn's encounters with indigenous communities along her journey offer insights into their culture and wisdom. These interactions expose her to a different way of life and provide her with valuable lessons about respect, tradition, and the importance of connection to the land.

As the journey progresses, Robyn's inner transformation becomes evident. She sheds layers of her past, confronts her own vulnerabilities, and finds strength in solitude and self-reliance. Through the solitude of the desert, she gains a deeper understanding of herself and her place in the world.

The movie concludes with Robyn's arrival at the ocean, the culmination of her arduous journey. As she dives into the water, a symbol of renewal and rebirth, she embraces the profound changes she has undergone. Her transformation is not limited to the physical completion of her trek but extends to a new outlook on life and a sense of empowerment.

The story of "Tracks" highlights the transformative power of a journey undertaken with purpose and determination. It illustrates how the challenges, solitude, and self-reflection inherent in a long and arduous journey can lead to personal growth, self-discovery, and a profound connection to oneself and the world. Robyn's trek becomes a metaphor for the transformative potential of any journey, emphasizing that the true value lies not in the destination but in the profound changes experienced along the way.

Lost and Found Ali

Ali, a student at Istanbul University, embarked on an eagerly anticipated month-long journey across Europe, ready to explore various cities. Little did he know that this adventure would be filled with unforeseen challenges, pushing him to learn valuable life lessons along the way.

His first destination was Paris, the enchanting city of lights. Arriving with excitement, Ali couldn't wait to immerse himself in the renowned art and cultural heritage. However, as he reached the entrance of the Louvre Museum, he realized with dismay that he had lost his ticket, which he had purchased online. Frustration washed over him, but he decided to seek help from a friendly local. With empathy, the local guided Ali to the museum's information desk, where he explained his situation. To Ali's surprise, the staff understood his predicament and managed to retrieve his ticket through the system, providing him with a replacement.

Next, Ali ventured to Vienna, the captivating capital of classical music. However, his excitement turned into disappointment when he discovered the high prices of concert tickets, making it challenging for him to attend a renowned performances. Expressing his frustration at the hostel, Ali struck up a conversation with a fellow traveler named Jonas. To his delight, Jonas informed him about the free street performances taking place in the city. Intrigued, Ali researched further and discovered that professional pianists were showcasing their talent on Kärntner Straße, allowing him to enjoy the enchanting melodies without financial constraints.

As Ali continued his journey, he arrived in Prague, a city renowned for its romantic ambiance and artistic atmosphere. While strolling through its captivating streets, he came across Kasia, a struggling artist selling her paintings. Intrigued by her melancholic expression, Ali struck up a conversation, uncovering her loss of inspiration and impending abandonment of her passion. Determined to reignite Kasia's creative spark, Ali proposed they explore Prague together. Throughout their explorations, Ali's genuine curiosity and appreciation for the city's beauty revitalized Kasia's spirit. The following day, Kasia invited Ali to her studio, where they spent meaningful time together. Witnessing Kasia create a breathtaking painting, Ali realized the power of human connection and the ability to inspire others.

Leaving Kasia behind was bittersweet for Ali, but he had to catch his train to Berlin. Excitement surged within him as he approached the iconic Brandenburg Gate. However, his enthusiasm was abruptly shattered when a pickpocketer snatched his wallet and passport just before he disembarked. Determined not to let this setback ruin his journey, Ali swiftly reported the incident to the police. Nevertheless, Ali found himself without a place to stay and no passport to board a plane. Desperation began to sink in, especially since the Turkish consulate was closed until Monday. In an act of kindness, the police officer took Ali to a Turkish cafe, hoping someone there could offer assistance. Approaching a Turkish family enjoying their coffee, Ali introduced himself and shared his story. Although they couldn't host him, they immediately contacted another Turkish student residing in Berlin for help. Additionally, they asked the cafe owner to provide Ali with food and drinks, ensuring his well-being.

Mehmet, the Turkish student living in Berlin, swiftly responded to the family's call for help and graciously hosted Ali that night. Their friendship blossomed during their time together. As they conversed, Mehmet shared insights about the German education system and the numerous educational opportunities available in Germany. Ali discovered that transferring to a university in Germany was rather easy and that education at German universities was tuition-free. This realization opened up new possibilities and broadened Ali's horizons.

With the Turkish consulate slow to assist him, Ali stayed with Mehmet for another five days. Eventually, on a Friday, he received confirmation that he could return to Turkey with a dream of continuing his studies in Germany.

Growing Through Journeys

Journeys have the incredible power to transform us, allowing us to grow and develop in ways we never imagined. Through travel, we embark on a path of self-discovery, broadening our perspectives, building resilience, and stepping out of our comfort zones. In this essay, we will explore seven ways in which journeys can foster personal growth and provide illustrative examples for each point.

One of the most profound ways journeys help us grow is by broadening our perspectives. When we step outside our familiar surroundings and immerse ourselves in new cultures, languages, and ways of life, we gain a deeper understanding of the world. For instance, traveling to a remote village in Cambodia and engaging with the locals can expose us to their daily struggles, creating empathy and appreciation for their resilience and resourcefulness. This expanded perspective encourages us to be more open-minded, accepting, and appreciative of diversity.

Journeys also allow us to build resilience, as they often present unforeseen challenges and obstacles. When we encounter setbacks or face unexpected situations, we learn to adapt and persevere. For example, trekking through the rugged terrain of the Himalayas can test our physical and mental limits, but by pushing through the difficulties and reaching the summit, we develop resilience and a sense of accomplishment that extends beyond the journey itself.

Self-discovery is another vital aspect of journeys. Stepping away from our everyday routines and immersing ourselves in new environments provides an opportunity for introspection and self-reflection. Consider a solo backpacking trip across Europe, where solitude and self-reliance become our constant companions. As we navigate unfamiliar cities, interact with diverse individuals, and spend time alone with our thoughts, we gain a deeper understanding of our own values, aspirations, and strengths.

Stepping out of our comfort zones is an inherent part of any journey, and it is through this discomfort that we experience personal growth. Venturing into the unknown and embracing new experiences can be transformative. For instance, participating in a homestay program in a remote village in Peru, where we are immersed in a different way of life, challenges our assumptions and forces us to adapt to unfamiliar customs and traditions. This step outside our comfort zones cultivates personal growth, self-confidence, and adaptability.

One of the invaluable outcomes of journeys is the development of cultural competence. By experiencing different cultures firsthand, we learn to appreciate and respect diversity. Imagine exploring the bustling streets of Marrakech, Morocco, where the sights, sounds, and aromas overwhelm your senses. Engaging with locals, haggling at vibrant markets, and participating in traditional rituals provide an immersive experience that fosters cultural understanding, empathy, and the ability to navigate cross-cultural interactions with sensitivity.

Journeys also enhance our problem-solving skills as we encounter unexpected challenges along the way. Whether it's navigating complex transportation systems, resolving language barriers, or adapting to unforeseen circumstances, we are forced to think on our feet and find creative solutions. For instance, missing a train connection in Tokyo may seem daunting, but by seeking assistance from locals, exploring alternative routes, and remaining calm under pressure, we develop problem-solving skills that prove invaluable in other areas of life.

Lastly, journeys foster independence and self-reliance. Traveling solo empowers us to take charge of our experiences, from planning itineraries to managing logistics and making decisions. Consider a backpacker exploring the rugged landscapes of New Zealand. With a map in hand and a sense of adventure, they navigate through breathtaking trails, camp under starlit skies, and make connections with fellow travelers. This independence builds self-confidence, resilience, and a sense of empowerment that extends beyond the journey itself.

Slow and Problematic Journeys

Journeys have long been recognized as transformative experiences that can enrich our lives and expand our horizons. However, not all journeys are created equal when it comes to learning and personal growth. In this essay, we will explore why slow journeys and journeys with problems offer unique advantages in fostering personal growth and development.

Slow Journeys

Slow journeys offer a distinct advantage over fast ones when it comes to learning and personal growth. Here are some reasons why slow journeys are better for learning:

Deep immersion:

Slow journeys allow for deeper immersion in the local culture, environment, and experiences. Spending more time in one place enables us to engage with the local community, learn their customs, and gain a deeper understanding of their way of life. By taking the time to connect with locals, participate in their daily activities, and build meaningful relationships, we enhance our cultural competence and broaden our perspectives.

Reflection and introspection:

Slow journeys provide ample opportunities for reflection and introspection. When we slow down our pace of travel, we have the time and space to process our experiences, reflect on our thoughts and emotions, and gain insights into ourselves. Whether it's journaling by a serene lake or meditating in a peaceful mountain retreat, these moments of introspection foster self-discovery and personal growth.

Immersive learning:

Slow journeys allow for immersive learning experiences. Whether it's learning a new language, taking cooking classes, or practicing traditional arts and crafts, spending an extended period in one place gives us the opportunity to delve deeper into local traditions and gain hands-on knowledge. This immersive learning allows us to develop new skills, broaden our intellectual horizons, and foster a deeper appreciation for different forms of knowledge.

Journeys with Problems

Let's explore why journeys with problems are often better for learning and growth compared to journeys without any issues:Journeys with problems build resilience, enhance problem-solving skills, and promote self-awareness.

Building resilience:

Journeys with problems challenge us to navigate through obstacles, adapt to unexpected situations, and find solutions. These challenges build resilience and strengthen our ability to cope with adversity. Overcoming difficulties fosters personal growth and equips us with valuable skills that extend beyond the journey itself.

Problem-solving skills:

Journeys with problems require us to think critically, analyze situations, and find creative solutions. Whether it's navigating a transportation mishap, resolving a language barrier, or managing unexpected delays, these challenges enhance our problem-solving skills and broaden our ability to think on our feet.

Learning from setbacks:

Journeys with problems provide valuable opportunities to learn from setbacks and failures. When things don't go according to plan, we have the chance to reflect on what went wrong, evaluate our choices, and identify areas for improvement. These setbacks offer valuable life lessons and enable personal growth through self-reflection and resilience-building.

Increased self-awareness:

Journeys with problems often push us out of our comfort zones and present us with new and unfamiliar situations. This heightened state of awareness and adaptability fosters self-awareness, as we discover our strengths, weaknesses, and areas for personal growth. It prompts us to reassess our beliefs, values, and priorities, leading to personal transformation and self-discovery.

The Camino de Santiago

The Camino de Santiago[21], also referred to as the Way of St. James, is a significant Christian pilgrimage route that culminates at the shrine of the apostle St. James in Santiago de Compostela, Spain. This pilgrimage holds deep spiritual and cultural importance for Christians around the world. Pilgrims embark on a transformative journey along various routes, with the Camino Francés being the most renowned and frequented.

The Camino de Santiago traces its origins back to the 9th century when the remains of St. James were believed to have been discovered in Santiago de Compostela. This discovery led to the establishment of a pilgrimage route, and over the centuries, the Camino grew in popularity, attracting pilgrims from different parts of Europe and beyond. Today, it continues to captivate the hearts and minds of countless individuals seeking spiritual enrichment and a deeper connection with their faith.

The pilgrimage experience on the Camino de Santiago is characterized by a combination of physical, emotional, and spiritual elements. Pilgrims undertake a challenging journey on foot, covering extensive distances that can span hundreds of kilometers. Walking the Camino allows pilgrims to embrace a slower pace of life, fostering self-reflection, contemplation, and a heightened sense of awareness.

The Camino de Santiago offers pilgrims a unique opportunity for spiritual growth and self-discovery. The physical exertion involved in the pilgrimage can be seen as a metaphor for life's challenges and the determination required to overcome them. Pilgrims often encounter moments of introspection, where they can delve into their own beliefs, values, and personal journeys. The solitude and tranquility of the Camino enable pilgrims to seek guidance, find solace, and connect with God on a deeply personal level.

---

[21] Eanes, Russ. The Walk of a Lifetime: 500 Miles on the Camino de Santiago. Amerika Birleşik Devletleri, Walker Press, 2019.

Along the way, pilgrims encounter a network of infrastructure and services developed specifically for their needs. Hostels, known as albergues, provide accommodation and foster a sense of community among fellow travelers. Pilgrims engage in shared meals, conversations, and experiences, forging meaningful connections and bonds with people from diverse backgrounds. This communal aspect reinforces the idea of a unified spiritual journey and highlights the importance of human connection in the pilgrimage experience.

The Camino de Santiago is not solely a religious pilgrimage; it is also a cultural and historical journey. Pilgrims traverse picturesque landscapes, pass through ancient towns and villages, and witness architectural marvels, such as Romanesque cathedrals and medieval bridges. These encounters with history, art, and culture contribute to a holistic and enriching experience.

In conclusion, the Camino de Santiago, or the Way of St. James, is a transformative Christian pilgrimage that invites individuals to embark on a profound journey of faith, reflection, and spiritual growth. As pilgrims walk the various routes leading to Santiago de Compostela, they engage in self-discovery, connect with their spirituality, and embrace the camaraderie of fellow travelers. The Camino de Santiago serves as a physical and metaphorical pathway towards a deeper understanding of one's beliefs, offering an opportunity for personal transformation and a renewed sense of purpose.

The Hajj: A Pillar of Islam and a Transformative Journey

The Hajj[22], one of the five pillars of Islam, holds great significance as a sacred pilgrimage for Muslims worldwide. It is a spiritual journey that Muslims undertake with profound devotion, seeking to fulfill their religious obligations and connect with the essence of their faith. The Hajj encompasses a range of rituals and practices that symbolize unity, submission, and personal transformation. In this essay, we will explore why the Hajj is considered one of the five pillars of Islam and delve into the historical aspects of the pilgrimage before the 19th century.

Before the 19th century, the rules and practices of Hajj (the annual Islamic pilgrimage to Mecca) were influenced by the historical context and the means of transportation available at the time. While the core rituals remained consistent, there were variations in the modes of travel and the journey itself. Here are some notable aspects of Hajj before the 19th century:

1. Traveling on Foot: With limited transportation options, the majority of pilgrims traveled to Mecca on foot. They embarked on long and arduous journeys, sometimes lasting several months, to reach the sacred city. Walking was considered a significant part of the pilgrimage experience, representing endurance, humility, and devotion.

2. Caravans: Due to the challenges of travel and the need for security, pilgrims often joined caravans for protection and companionship. These caravans would consist of fellow believers from their region or tribe, facilitating a sense of community and mutual support during the journey. Traveling together also helped in sharing resources, such as food, water, and shelter.

---

[22] Peters, F. E.. The Hajj: The Muslim Pilgrimage to Mecca and the Holy Places. Birleşik Krallık, Princeton University Press, 2021.

3. Slow and Deliberate Journey: The journey to Mecca was usually slow and deliberate, allowing pilgrims to engage in acts of worship, reflection, and spiritual preparation. It provided an opportunity for self-discipline, self-reflection, and detachment from worldly concerns. The journey itself was seen as an essential part of the pilgrimage experience, fostering personal growth and a sense of unity among the pilgrims.

4. Staying in Waystations and Resting Areas: Along the pilgrimage routes, there were designated waystations and resting areas where pilgrims could take a break, seek shelter, and replenish their supplies. These stations provided a temporary refuge, allowing pilgrims to rest and recover before continuing their journey.

5. Hospitality and Support: Local communities along the pilgrimage routes played a crucial role in providing hospitality and support to the pilgrims. They would offer food, water, and shelter to the weary travelers, considering it a virtuous act of service. This tradition of hospitality continues to this day, with local residents in Mecca and Medina opening their homes to pilgrims during Hajj.

6. Spiritual Preparation: Pilgrims would engage in various acts of spiritual preparation before undertaking the journey. This included repentance, seeking forgiveness, and resolving any outstanding disputes or debts. The intention and mindset of the pilgrim were considered important, as Hajj was seen as a sacred obligation and an opportunity for spiritual transformation.

Chapter Summary

Journeys, full of challenges and uncertainties, serve as profound catalysts for personal transformation. These adventures push us to the brink, revealing our qualities, strengthening our resilience, and enhancing our adaptability. The significant impact of these journeys lies in their ability to humble us, make us appreciate the power of seeking and extending help, and stimulate personal growth. They also broaden our perspectives through exposure to various cultures and lifestyles, force us out of our comfort zones, sharpen our problem-solving skills, and foster independence. By doing so, journeys prepare us to seize second chances, steering us towards a path of self-improvement and personal development.

Chapter Lessons

1. Humility: Journeys teach us to acknowledge our insignificance in the grand scheme of things, fostering humility and compassion.

2. Resilience and Adaptability: They test our ability to withstand adversities and adapt to new circumstances, thereby enhancing our resilience and adaptability.

3. Value of Assistance: We learn to appreciate the importance of seeking help when needed and extending it to others in times of distress.

4. Broadened Perspectives: Exposure to diverse cultures and lifestyles provides us with a deeper understanding of the world, encouraging us to be more accepting and appreciative of diversity.

5. Stepping Out of Comfort Zones: Journeys often involve venturing into unfamiliar territories, forcing us to step out of our comfort zones and enhancing personal growth, self-confidence, and adaptability.

6. Problem-Solving Skills: They put us in unexpected situations, requiring us to think on our feet and develop creative solutions.

7. Independence: Traveling, especially solo, fosters independence and self-reliance, enhancing self-confidence and resilience.

8. Personal Growth: The sum total of these experiences leads to significant personal growth, equipping us to seize second chances and transform our lives.

Conclusion

In this book, our journey through the realms of second chances, self-worth, surmounting trauma, acceptance, outreach, fresh starts, belief in miracles, and the transformative influence of journeys, has unveiled a rich blend of insights, experiences, and life lessons. The stories and anecdotes I have shared reflect a common human ability to learn, grow, and transform, no matter our life situations or past choices. As the old saying goes, it's never too late to become the person you might have been.

In my exploration of second chances in the first chapter, I've unveiled how opportunities can be grasped, wasted, or unnoticed. I've discovered that each moment gifts us the potential for a fresh start, a turn, or a leap.

Yet, whether we notice or harness these opportunities largely depends on our sense of self-worth, as discussed in the second chapter. Feeling valued and fostering self-confidence are crucial elements in gathering the bravery to tread a new path or enact significant life changes.

Chapter three allowed me to examine the role of surmounting and facing trauma in shaping our second chances. As I've learned, trauma can act as an obstacle to progress, but with the right approaches, it can be alleviated, navigated, and ultimately conquered.

During the process of creating and seizing second chances, as highlighted in chapter four, accepting our realities, flaws, and errors, as well as reaching out for help, are crucial. These actions, though seemingly straightforward, demand great courage and humility, and can greatly influence our capacity to transform our lives.

Chapter five illuminated the invaluable role that newcomers - whether friends, colleagues, pets, neighbors, or relatives - play in our lives. They introduce fresh perspectives, joy, and opportunities for growth, fostering an environment that's ripe for second chances.

In chapter six, I explored the power of believing in miracles, emphasizing the importance of maintaining positivity and hope, even in the face of adversity.

Finally, in chapter seven, we discovered how journeys, both literal and metaphorical, can serve as powerful catalysts for change, equipping us with resilience, adaptability, and life lessons essential for personal transformation.

In conclusion, this book, and principles within have been a compass for me, guiding me through the diverse landscapes of personal growth and transformation.

It stands as a testament to our shared human potential to rise above our pasts, seize our present, and shape our desired future.

The essence of life's second chances isn't always about starting from scratch; sometimes, it's about pushing forward, believing in our capabilities, and creating a triumphant narrative against all odds. I hope that the stories, principles, and lessons shared here inspire and motivate you to seize your second chance when it arrives and to navigate your journey with resilience, courage, and hope.

Special Thanks

I am immensely grateful to my extraordinary students in the Second Chance course. Thank you for your unwavering commitment, perseverance, and boundless enthusiasm. Your dedication has been truly inspiring. Your courage in confronting your issues, your willingness to learn from them, and your dedication to creating a better future are what make this program and book truly transformative. Each of your stories has enriched this course and book and inspired not just me but all those around you.

A heartfelt thank you to Necdet Buyukbay, whose unwavering support and motivation played a significant role in the creation of this program. Your belief in learning was infectious, and your encouragement helped turn this program from a dream into a reality. I am deeply grateful for your trust.

I also want to express my deepest gratitude to Betul, my former assistant. Her tireless efforts in summarizing the movies and creating the basis for this book have been instrumental in shaping the course and the book. Her commitment, dedication, and hard work have truly made a difference.

In this transformative journey, a gathering of inspiring individuals has played a pivotal role, and for this, my gratitude knows no bounds. These are the people who have forged their own second chances, embodying the core essence of this program through their unwavering strength, tenacity, and belief in the power of redemption. Without their seamless contributions, this book would not have seen the light of day.

Sources

1. Field of Dreams. Directed by Phil Alden Robinson, Universal Pictures, 1989.

2. In America. Directed by Jim Sheridan, Miramax Films, 2002.

3. Ashley, Greg C., and Roni Reiter-Palmon. "Self-awareness and the evolution of leaders: The need for a better measure of self-awareness." Journal of Behavioral and Applied Management, vol. 14, no. 1, 2012, pp. 2-17.

4. Eurich, Tasha. "What self-awareness really is (and how to cultivate it)." Harvard Business Review, vol. 4, 2018.

5. Saxena, Parul. "Johari Window: An effective model for improving interpersonal communication and managerial effectiveness." SIT Journal of Management, vol. 5, no. 2, 2015, pp. 134-146.

6. The World's Fastest Indian. Directed by Roger Cox, Fox Searchlight Pictures, 2005.

7. The Straight Story. Directed by David Lynch, Buena Vista Pictures Distribution, 1999.

8. The Kid. Directed by Jon Turteltaub, Touchstone Pictures, 2000.

9. Shall We Dance. Directed by Peter Chelsom, Miramax Films, 2004.

10. Bell, Michael Mayerfeld. "The ghosts of place." Theory and society, vol. 26, no. 6, 1997, pp. 813-836.

11. Lambert, Michael J., Allen E. Bergin, and S. L. Garfield. "The effectiveness of psychotherapy." Encyclopedia of psychotherapy, vol. 1, 1994, pp. 709-714.

12. Handbook of Exposure Therapies. Edited by David CS Richard, and Dean Lauterbach, Elsevier, 2011.

13. Turner, Rhonda, and Susan M. Swearer Napolitano. "Cognitive behavioral therapy (CBT)." 2010.

14. Smith, Jonathan C. Relaxation, Meditation, & Mindfulness: A Mental Health Practitioner's Guide to New and Traditional Approaches. Springer Publishing Company, 2005.

15. Forrest, M. S., Shapiro, F. EMDR: The Breakthrough "Eye Movement" Therapy For Overcoming Anxiety, Stress, And Trauma. Basic Books, 2004.

16. Gideon. Directed by Claudia Hoover, MGM, 1998.

17. Finding Forrester. Directed by Gus Marshall, Touchstone Pictures, 2000.

18. Because of Winn-Dixie. Directed by Wayne Wang, 20th Century Fox, Walden Media, 2005.

19. Himalaya: L'Enfance d'un chef. Directed by Éric Valli, Pathé Renn Productions, 1999.

20. Tracks. Directed by John Curran, Roadshow Entertainment, 2013.

21. Eanes, Russ. The Walk of a Lifetime: 500 Miles on the Camino de Santiago. Walker Press, 2019.

22. Peters, F. E. The Hajj: The Muslim Pilgrimage to Mecca and the Holy Places. Princeton University Press, 2021.